William Francis Finlason, Edward J. Eyre, Colin Blackburn

Report of the Case of the Queen v. Edward John Eyre

on his prosecution, in the Court of Queen's bench, for high crimes and misdemeanours alleged to have been committed by him in his office as governor of Jamaica

William Francis Finlason, Edward J. Eyre, Colin Blackburn

Report of the Case of the Queen v. Edward John Eyre

on his prosecution, in the Court of Queen's bench, for high crimes and misdemeanours alleged to have been committed by him in his office as governor of Jamaica

ISBN/EAN: 9783337331665

Printed in Europe, USA, Canada, Australia, Japan

Cover: Foto ©Suzi / pixelio.de

More available books at **www.hansebooks.com**

REPORT

OF THE CASE OF

THE QUEEN v. EDWARD JOHN EYRE,

ON HIS PROSECUTION,

In the Court of Queen's Bench,

FOR HIGH CRIMES AND MISDEMEANOURS ALLEGED TO HAVE
BEEN COMMITTED BY HIM IN HIS OFFICE AS

GOVERNOR OF JAMAICA;

CONTAINING

THE EVIDENCE, (TAKEN FROM THE DEPOSITIONS),
THE INDICTMENT,

AND

THE CHARGE OF MR. JUSTICE BLACKBURN.

BY

W. F. FINLASON, ESQ.,
Barrister-at-Law.

LONDON:
CHAPMAN AND HALL, PICCADILLY,
AND
STEVENS & SON, 24, BELL YARD, LINCOLN'S INN.
MDCCCLXVIII.

LONDON:
BURT, SIEVENS, AND CO.,
WINE OFFICE COURT, FLEET STREET.

CONTENTS.

	PAGES.
I. THE EVIDENCE TAKEN FROM THE DEPOSITIONS	1 to 32
II. THE INDICTMENT	33 to 52
III. THE CHARGE	53 to 102

Just published,

A REVIEW OF THE AUTHORITIES

AS TO THE

REPRESSION OF RIOT AND REBELLION,

And as to the Criminal or Civil Responsibility of those engaged in such Repression; comprising Notices of all the Statutes and Cases on the Subject.

INTRODUCTION.

The prosecution of a Colonial Governor, in the Court of Queen's Bench, for high crimes and misdemeanours alleged to have been committed, in the exercise of his office, by the abuse of his powers for the purpose of oppression, is an event happily of so rare occurrence in our history, that it deserves some record; and the exposition of the law on the subject, upon such an occasion, by an able and learned judge, must be worth preserving. And as in this instance the alleged abuse had been committed in the course of the execution of measures represented to be required for the suppression of rebellion, the subject has a special interest with reference to its bearing on the powers and responsibilities of magistrates or still higher functionaries in the repression of riot and insurrection; while it has a peculiar interest on this further account, that it laid down the law with results entirely different from those arrived at on the occasion of a former prosecution arising out of the same matters, and on which a charge had been delivered and published by the Lord Chief Justice.

There was a general feeling in the profession that the Charge of Mr. Justice Blackburn ought to be published, and it is here presented exactly as the learned judge delivered it, with the exception of his mere verbal corrections. The writer would have desired to present it by itself with the addition of no other matter than the Evidence and the Indictment presented to the grand jury and upon which the charge was pronounced. And therefore it is in a separate form he has prepared a Review of the Authorities, in which it will be seen how closely the learned judge has adhered to the law upon the subject: and also a history of the Jamaica case, which has been the subject of so much discussion, and of such repeated prosecutions. Nor would he have added a word more, but for the unfortunate attempt made by the Lord Chief Justice to disparage the authority of the charge of his learned brother and to uphold that of his own, which has made it necessary, in justice not merely to the learned judge, but to the profession and the public (not to say anything of the parties more immediately affected), to consider the grounds on which the present charge is supposed to be impeached, and to point out the considerations with reference to which the comparative weight or authority of the two charges may be appreciated and understood.

Now although in a certain sense a charge to a grand jury is not an authority in the fullest sense of a *judicial decision* of the law, yet on the other hand, a careful exposition of the law, by an able and learned judge on an important subject, and on a great occasion, is not only likely to be valuable, but may have a very large amount of authority in the sense of a well-considered and responsible *declaration* of the law. But then this is subject to two cardinal conditions. The one is, that it applies only to the declaration of *matters of law:* and the other is, that these matters shall be *relevant.* For there is one invariable and essential element of judicial authority: that it attaches only in the discharge of a judicial duty: and therefore it can never attach to what is said beyond the scope of such judicial duty, and of course still less to what is said in *disregard* of it. Now the province of the judge is *matter of law*, and it is *especially* so in a *criminal case*, and it is so peculiarly in a charge to a grand jury, which is necessarily upon *ex parte* statements and an imperfect case. On such an occasion the judicial duty is clear and simple, and its *limits* plain and strict. It is simply a duty to direct the grand jury upon the matters of law essential or material for the due discharge of *their* function, which is the *application* of the law to facts. That is to give them clear, plain, positive direction upon the matters of law which appear to be involved in the offences alleged in the indictment presented, and to leave the matters of fact for their determination, on the evidence, by the light of this declaration of the law. It is expected of the judge that he shall fulfil his own function, it is not permitted to him to go beyond it, and encroach upon theirs. He *does* so encroach if he enters into the facts, and seeks to enforce his own impressions of them. It is *unlawful* for him to do so, and if he does so, especially if he does so to the prejudice of the accused he does an act as distinctly *illegal* as any offence with which the accused may be charged. The reason is obvious, that the attempt by a powerful and cultivated mind, to enforce its own views of the facts upon others must necessarily exercise some influence, and that influence, if exercised adversely to the accused, that is to convey a view or impression of the facts unfavourable to him, is an unlawful injury to him, because especially upon this *exparte* and imperfect statement of the case he is entitled in law to the *unbiassed* judgment of the grand jury, and to the extent to which they are influenced by the judge upon the facts, he is illegally injured, and deprived of a legal right. To which it may be added, that if a judge were allowed thus to enter into the facts, then, in any case on which he happened to have formed a strong opinion upon them, there would be great danger of his unconsciously conveying his own view or version of them *instead* of the real and actual facts, and of substituting his own impressions, or even imaginations, for the verities of the *evidence*. And it is manifest that in proportion as the occasion was one which had given rise to much public discussion, and was one which had engaged men's minds and excited opposite opinions and feelings, the danger would be the greater of preconceived views and impressions, and therefore the reason would be stronger for a rigid adherence to the established rule that the judge has no right to enter into the matters of fact.

What a charge to a grand jury in a serious criminal case should be, and what it always *had* been (at least in modern times), had been, not long before these unhappy events, admirably illustrated, in the charge delivered by that able judge, Mr. Justice Keogh, on the occasion of the prosecution in 1865 under the Treason Felony Act, which makes penal any acts or attempts with intent to levy war against the Crown. And as some passages in that charge bear closely upon the present subject, they may be usefully extracted here as of high judicial authority. It will be seen that they are clear, positive directions upon *matters of law*, and the matters of law involved in the case before him. Having read and explained the Act, the learned judge went on to explain the nature of the offence:—

> "The crime with which the parties stand charged, is an attempt to depose the Queen, or with the intent to levy war with a view to compel her by force to change her measures or counsels, or with intent to stir up foreigners or strangers to invade this country; but though the intent is of the essence of the crime, that intent must be attested or indicated by the *publishing of some printing or writing*, or by some other overt act or deed. It *may* be attested by *any* act or deed, but it must be attested *either* by the publishing of some *printing or writing*, or by some overt act or deed, before the prisoner can be found guilty of the offence with which he is charged."

Then the learned judge went on to explain the nature of the evidence which it required, and, on the other hand, the nature of the evidence which would be sufficient:—

> "Now, gentlemen, as to the first of these tests—the publishing, the printing or writing—if they are charged, and I believe they are in the indictment to be sent before you, it is my duty to tell you that you are bound, in the first place, to see that the publication is proved *prima facie* and brought home to the accused; and, secondly, when they are proved and brought home to the accused, that they do, in fact, *indicate the guilty intent* with which the accused stands charged."

Here it is plainly conveyed to the grand jury that

a treasonable intent might be collected from the contents of papers published, and their natural tendency :—

"So long as these publications do not travel into the region of force and lawless violence, a British jury cannot, in my opinion, be too indulgent. But, gentlemen, if, transcending these limits, not alone by the violence of expression, but *by the matter and substance of their suggestions*, they assail the time-honoured fabric of our constitution, aiming, with parricidal hand, to destroy the bonds which bind in one family these British islands—*Sceleris crimen parricidii furoris*—then, *not only are you right, but justified*, in my opinion, in the conscientious discharge of your duty, *to attach to the publication the criminal intent* which the indictment charges, and so find a true bill, and send the case forward for further investigation. So much as to publishing in print or writing."

Here it will be observed that it was only in the event of the grand jury being satisfied that the offence had been committed that they were to send the case on for further investigation. And no trace is to be found of the monstrous doctrine recently propounded that a grand jury are warranted in finding a true bill, although *not* satisfied that the offence has been committed, in order that it may be sent for further investigation. The established doctrine had always been, and is here adhered to, that the grand jury are not warranted in finding a bill unless upon the evidence, unanswered, a jury, on the trial, must find the accused guilty. Then upon the law as to all the acts or elements which might be involved in the offence the learned judge gave clear, plain, positive directions. Thus, for instance, as to *conspiracy* :—

"A conspiracy may exist whenever two or more persons combine together to commit any illegal offence, or to effect even any legal purpose by illegal means. If, in the course of your inquiries, the existence of any such conspiracy as may be charged in the indictment as an overt act, especially *prima facie* overt, is brought home, either existing amongst themselves alone, or any of them with any other persons, then I have to tell you, gentlemen, that every act and declaration of each member of the confederacy in pursuance of the original plan, and with reference to the common object, may be given in evidence against them, or any one of them—and this without reference to the time at which the party might have joined the confederacy, or whether the act was done in his presence or not, or in the same place in which he was or not. Time or distance make no distinction in the case, as the law amounts to this, that if a man once agree with others to effect a common illegal purpose, every act which either had before been done, or may afterwards be done, by any of his confederates in furtherance of the common design, may be given in evidence against him."

So, again, as to the important point of law which lies at the basis of the present subject of martial law, but to which, it will be seen, the Lord Chief Justice in his charge never adverted, viz., that rebellion is levying war against the Crown, and that it may be constructive, and does not require *military* arming or array—a doctrine the foundation of our whole law of treason, and laid down by all our great Crown lawyers—the learned judge said :—

"The words 'levy war' you have already heard me read to you from t Act, and frequently used, and I have explained that you are only concerned with the intent to levy, as no *actual* levying of war is charged in the indictment. You must be satisfied with the intent, but *to constitute the offence it is not necessary that war, with all the pomp and circumstance of military array, should exist.* Nothing of the kind. *Any armed insurrection, however small or ill-managed, for the purpose of subverting the constitution by force and numbers, would constitute a levying of war,* and to compass or intend any such rising would make the offence charged in this indictment."

Having given the grand jury these plain, clear, positive directions on the matters of law, the learned judge left to them the *application* of the law to the facts, not himself entering into the evidence at all :—

"Gentlemen, you will bear this instruction in mind when you *come to apply the evidence to the cases before you.* As to all these, or any of them, you will apply yourselves in a firm, but at the same time, I say, a fair and liberal spirit, and *say, upon your oaths, if they are proved and brought home to the accused,* do they or any of them indicate the intentions with which the prisoners are charged ? If they do, it will be your duty to find the bill—if not it will be equally your duty to ignore it. I have said that all these matters depend upon the evidence to be produced; what that evidence is likely to be, I know not, but, as I have before told you, a conspiracy to dethrone the sovereign, or by force to subvert the constitution, or to levy war, or incite foreigners to invade this country, may be properly charged and given in evidence as an overt act, and indicating the different felonious intentions in this Act of Parliament."

INTRODUCTION. vii

The learned judge, in conclusion, distinctly declined to enter into the evidence, *lest he should prejudice the prisoners or prejudge the case*, and he declared it to be the practice of great judges so to abstain:—

"I have now closed all I intend to address to you for your guidance in matters of law. Now, as to the facts and circumstances connected with the treasonable designs charged against the prisoners, *I forbear to enter upon them, even to the limited extent to which they are known to me through the sworn informations. I do so deliberately. I do so following the example of one of the greatest judges who ever sat on the English bench, Lord Ellenborough, who at a moment of great public excitement, declined in his address to the grand jury to go into any details of the offences, lest by any words of his he might in the slightest degree prejudice the case, either of the Crown or the prisoners.*"

Such was the view which that able judge took of the province and function of a judge in charging a grand jury, and such his testimony as to the usage handed down by the distinguished judges who had occupied the chair of Chief Justice of the King's Bench.

There was, however, after this a still more recent illustration of the views and the usage of judges upon this point, and it was one afforded in the course of the prosecution arising out of the very matters now in hand. For not long before the Lord Chief Justice delivered his charge, a learned judge in Jamaica had charged a grand jury, in a case which occurred during the existence of martial law (a case which formed one of the heads of accusation against Mr. Eyre in the present prosecution), on a charge of murder against the Provost-marshal for the summary execution of a man without trial and without orders. It would be impossible to imagine a stronger case, nor one more likely to excite the feelings; and yet the learned judge, Mr. Justice Ker, adhered (perhaps on that very account) most closely and carefully to his legal province and function, of the matter of law; and he confined himself strictly to a calm, clear, positive direction upon the general nature and object of martial law, and the principles upon which criminal liability for acts done during martial law must depend.

It would be impossible to conceive anything more colourless or more clear. The learned Judge entirely abstained from entering into the evidence; and lest he should do so, having laid down a few leading principles, he confined himself to *reading the evidence.* Then he went on to say :—

"Cases are judged rather by their own peculiar circumstances than by reference to *more than a few leading rules and principles.* Nor will the law scrutinise too minutely particular acts, if only without violating any of the above-mentioned rules and principles, they forwarded, or tended to forward, the great end of martial law, the suppression of armed outbreak. This is not the place to discuss such a question, but it is manifest in the interest of those under its care, that every Government, whatever its form may be, must possess the power of resorting to force in the last extremity. The want of such a power would place the very existence of the State at the mercy of organised conspiracy. The public safety, therefore, which is the ultimate law, confides to the supreme authority in every country the power to declare it when the emergency has arisen. But martial law—and I desire to draw your particular attention to what I am going to observe—although, as I have stated, it dispenses with the forms and delays which appertain to the ordinary criminal jurisprudence, does not, therefore, authorise or sanction every deed assumed to be done in its name. It stops far short of that. For, if it did not, lawless men, under colour and putting forward the pretence of authority, might commit acts abhorrent to every principle of humanity. They might gratify malice and revenge, hatred and ill-will, lust and rapacity. They might perpetrate deeds from which the sun would hide its face. No greater error exists than to suppose that the subjecting of a district to the military power authorises excess on the part of those who administer that power. Deeply is it, therefore, in the interest of the public welfare, and in the interest of humanity, that it should be clearly understood what martial law sanctions, and what it does not. It allows, in one word, everything that is necessary towards putting down actual resistance to lawful authority. But this is not the only restraint which it imposes upon those who have the carrying of it out. It further requires that the acts of its ministers should be honest and *bona fide.* They must be done in good faith, or they will be disavowed. And, as a still further requisition, it fastens as a condition upon its agents that their acts shall be adjudged to be necessary in the judgment, not of a violent or excited, but of a moderate and reasonable man. Reason and common sense must approve the particular act. It is not sufficient that the party should unaffectedly believe such and such a line of conduct to be called for—the belief must be reasonably entertained, and such as a person of ordinary understanding would not repudiate. If these conditions are not fulfilled the act becomes simply unlawful, with all the consequences attaching to illegality. The moment that it ceases to be necessary for the suppression of armed revolt, that moment it loses its legal character. It then takes rank with those acts to which the privilege and protection of martial law are not extended. The vindictive passions are prohibited their exercise as absolutely and peremptorily during military rule as in the most orderly and tranquil condition of human affairs. Excess and wantonness, cruelty and unscrupulous contempt for human life, meet with no sanction from martial law any more than from ordinary law. No amount of personal provocation can justify or excuse vindictive retaliation. Were it otherwise, an institution which, though stern, is beneficial, would degenerate into an instrument of mere private malice and revenge."

Taking the whole scope of the direction, it will be seen that it came to this, exactly in accordance with the direction in Wall's case (28 State Trials, and Wright *v.* Fitzgerald, 27 State Trials), that the question was not whether the act was, in the judgment of the jury, strictly necessary, but whether, in their judgment, it might honestly, at the moment, have been thought to be so by a man of ordinary sense, but placed in an extraordinary emergency. And then, at the end, the question was thus clearly put to the grand jury :—

"The question, therefore, for your consideration will be, whether the Crown, upon the evidence which will be laid before you, have raised such a *prima facie* case against the accused, as to render it proper that the case should be remitted for the fuller inquiry which it necessarily receives at the trial."

As to this, it must be kept in mind that the act was *personally ordered by the prisoner*, on his own responsibility, and that, on the evidence for the prosecution, there was no provocation, nor any pretence of excuse or justification; yet, even in such a case, the strongest language the learned judge brought himself to utter was this :—

"Upon this subject I owe it to the administration of justice to remark that you ought not to have a doubt. *If these witnesses speak the truth*, they have told a tale which no system of criminal jurisprudence but is under a positive obligation to investigate. I need scarcely observe, that by finding a true bill you do not pronounce the defendant guilty, but merely call upon him to say what he has to urge by way of defence or explanation."

The province of the judge, therefore, being matter of law, and his function, even as to the law, being confined to such matters of law as are *relevant* to the offence charged ; there can be no difficulty, holding firmly to this test, in distinguishing the degree of judicial authority to be attributed to the charges now in question with reference to the subject of martial law or the measures legal or allowable for the suppression of rebellion.

In the case of the Queen *v.* Nelson, in which the Lord Chief Justice charged the Grand Jury at the Central Criminal Court, the crime charged was *murder;* i.e. in directing the execution of an alleged illegal sentence and execution by military men, under martial law and under the orders of a military superior : and the duty of the Lord Chief Justice, therefore, was to direct the grand jury as to the *law of murder* in its bearing on such a case. The main question was the law of *murder,* especially as to the doctrine set up of a sort of constructive murder by reason of the assumed illegality. The subject of martial law, it is manifest, was only involved collaterally, and only so far as it affected the particular case of the accused, and the question of its legality could not directly arise ; for, assuming its legality, still, as had been judicially held in that very court (in the case of Governor Wall) there might be evidence of felonious malice or a murderous mind ; and, on the other hand, assuming illegality, there might be evidence of such colour of legality and such honesty of belief in it as would take away all pretence of that felonious malice which must be of the essence of the crime of murder. If, therefore, the Lord Chief Justice had been able to give them a clear and positive direction, either that martial law was legal or illegal, or would be legal under some circumstances and illegal under others, that would be all he had to say about it, and he would then have had to give the governing direction in either view as to *felonious malice*. The direction would be, that in a given state of circumstances, as a rebellion, martial law could or could *not* be legal, leaving the grand jury to determine, on such direction, whether there *was* a rebellion. All that would be matter of law, beyond, would be the general nature of martial law as the law of war, or the general definition of a state of rebellion, and the proposition that it did or did not allow of martial law, leaving the application to them. And the particular nature of martial law, as to what it admits or allows, would, assuming it to be the law of war, not be matter of law, (as the courts know nothing of the laws of war), but matter of military usage, and understanding that matter of fact to be proved to the grand jury by cogent military authority. Though, on the other hand, if it could be brought within common or statute law, as, if it were regular military law, it would be, of course it would be, for the judge distinctly to state what it was—as matter of law : and again, to leave the practical *application* to the grand jury.

But if the Lord Chief Justice was *not* able to *instruct* the grand jury clearly upon the question of the legality of martial law, then, again, his province was to direct them clearly as to the law of murder, with reference to a case of *doubtful* legality, either, first, on the hypothesis of honesty, or, secondly, on the hypothesis of dishonesty. And this was exactly the case which practically presented itself on the occasion ; for the Lord Chief Justice was *not* able to give a distinct direction as to the legality or illegality of martial law, neither was he able to lay down any proposition of law on *any* of these points. He neither laid down, as matter of law, what martial law was, nor whether or not it was allowed in time of rebellion, in the sense in which it was understood and exercised by the accused. He *argued* that it was regular military law, under the Mutiny Acts and Articles of War (which, however, expressly apply only to those in the service of the Crown) ; and then upon that he expounded these enactments (as, upon that view, he would, of course, be right in doing), and asked the jury "why, if that be martial law as to soldiers, should it not be so as to civilians?"(p. 99). But he did not lay down that it *was* so; and, on the other hand, he laid down things which showed that it was *not* so—as, that rebel prisoners might be executed without trial, if taken after battle, which is not in the Articles of War, and would clearly not be legal at *common* law; so that he left the matter entirely in confusion. So, as to what would authorise or allow of martial law in either sense, as regular or irregular military law, the Lord Chief Justice gave no direction, and laid down no proposition of law. He never even adverted to the cardinal principle upon which, of course, the legality of martial law, or *lex martialis*, the law of war, must necessarily turn, viz., that *rebellion is war;* and thus, of course, gave no definition of such rebellion as would amount to war, nor of such acts of aiding or abetting as would render a man liable, as a soldier, for engaging in such rebellious war. Nor, indeed, could he be expected to do so upon his view of the facts, which he conveyed as strongly as he could to the jury—viz., that there had been *no rebellion.*

"The moment the soldiers appeared in the field the whole insurrection collapsed; a small military force was able *at once* to suppress the outbreak" (p. 6).

Thus the Lord Chief Justice told the jury, in effect, that there was no rebellion, but a mere outbreak of insurrection put down in a day (as he stated in a note); and, of course, if that were so there could be no need for martial law. That, however, was a question of fact for the jury, even if there was any evidence that the rebellion was at an end, which there was not, the evidence only being that there was no further outbreak at the particular place where it broke out, *which was in the occupation of troops.* Having, however, thus concluded the question of fact on which the whole question turned, the Lord Chief Justice left no ground for any declaration of the *law* as to rebellion; and any opinion he threw out on the question was entirely extra-judicial and of no judicial authority: first, because it was not warranted by the evidence before him; and next, because it was entirely irrelevant on the view he took of the facts. He only *argued* that a civilian in rebellion could not be liable to martial law, unless he happened to be taken in arms in or after battle, which, of course, would exclude all who had borne arms if they were not actually taken under these circumstances, and thus, also, would exclude all rebellions in which there was no "battle." No legal principle was laid down on which to base these views, but they were only arguments which left all unsettled; and thus this part of the subject was left in confusion. And as to the construction of local acts allowing martial law, there was no positive direction, and, in short, the whole of the general matters of law were *left to the jury*. It is curious that the strongest expression of his opinion was upon a matter of law *not involved in the case* before him, therefore entirely irrelevant, immaterial, and extra-judicial, as to the removal of a person into a district under martial law. The Lord Chief Justice himself said that this could not affect the legality of the *trial* there, supposing it otherwise legal. Whence it clearly followed that, as the prosecution was *against those who tried* the man, it could not be material whether the *removal* into the district was legal; and, therefore, any expression of opinion upon it by the Lord Chief Justice was irrelevant and extra-judicial; and, as it was seriously prejudicial to the Governor, it was utterly illegal and unjustifiable; and it need hardly be said that what is illegal and unjustifiable cannot possibly carry with it the least semblance of judicial authority. And the Lord Chief Justice laid down no proposition of law that a man cannot even be removed into a district under martial law for the purpose of trial for offences alleged to have been committed there. Possibly he may have been aware that it was held, after the Revolution, in

Lundy's case, that a man might, (without any statutory authority) be seized in this country in time of peace, and sent over to Ireland to be tried there, under martial law, for not defending a fortress against rebels or enemies, an offence capital there, though here at that time it would not have been so.* And he may have remembered Kimberley's case in the time of George II., when a man was sent over to Ireland, and tried and executed there for an offence not capital in this country.† And he probably knew that not long before his charge an eminent and learned judge, Mr. Justice Willes, had with great consideration held that an officer might be carried a thousand miles from Calcutta to Rangoon, to be tried by court-martial there for an offence committed there (though he might have been tried at Calcutta), because, as the learned Judge said—

"It is a general rule and principle that crime is local in its trial, and that offences are to be tried where they are alleged to have been committed: a principle of universal application."‡

At all events, the Lord Chief Justice did not lay down as a general rule or principle, contrary to this, that a man could not be removed into a district under martial law for the purpose of trial there. But he confined himself to the expression of a very strong opinion that the removal of *Gordon* was altogether unlawful and unjustifiable (Charge, p. 116)—a very different proposition, a *particular* proposition applied to the particular case, and either assuming a general principle or rule which had not been laid down, or assuming an *exceptional* ground not expressed, unless indeed it is to be found in the statement that the Governor took him to the district:—

"Took him from a district where there was no martial law and where he was safe, to a district where there was martial law, and where a military tribunal could be found *to try and condemn him!*" (p. 14).

This, it will be admitted, was a statement of a conclusion of fact, indeed a complex conclusion of fact, involving several

---

* 2 Ventris Reports, 314.   † 2 Strange's Reports, 848.
‡ Keighley v. Bell, 4 Foster and Finlason's Reports, 790.

matters of fact, as to which the Lord Chief Justice stated no evidence to support his conclusion, nor mentioned evidence before him which went to disprove it;* viz., that the Governor had desired the military commander to examine if there was sufficient evidence against the accused, and to try him *if it was proper* so to do. The Lord Chief Justice himself showed this was irrelevant, for he went on to say that the illegality or irregularity of the arrest would not affect the legality of the trial (p. 119). So that all he said upon it was utterly irrelevant.

But whether it was so or not, and whether he was right or wrong in his view, *it was not a matter of law;* for it depended, in the absence of any general and inflexible rule, (which he did not venture to lay down), upon the circumstances of the particular case, and its real character, which was for the jury. As this was the only point upon which the Lord Chief Justice expressed any decided difference from the law as laid down by Mr. Justice Blackburn, viz., that the removal of a man into the district under martial law *might* be lawful under proper circumstances—which was a proposition of law—it is important to point out, that neither on this nor on any other point did the Lord Chief Justice lay down any counter proposition of law; and therefore, though his dissent was conveyed in language which probably produced an impression upon the popular mind that there was a difference in law or legal principle, there was in reality no such difference, or, at all events, if there was, the Lord Chief Justice would not assume the responsibility of declaring it, and of laying down as a rule of law a proposition opposed to that which Mr. Justice Blackburn had so distinctly declared. Upon none of the great questions of law which were in his view involved in the case did the Lord Chief Justice venture to lay down any proposition of law. At the close he declared he was in doubt, and

---

* Colonel Nelson's Evidence (Minutes of Evidence, pp. 622—628), which had been put in on the part of the prosecution.

left the question to the jury with no other direction than this: that if they also should be in doubt as to the law (as of course they would be after such an avowal of doubt on his part), they should *find the bill for murder, in order to have the question settled;* that is, to present a man on their oaths for wilful murder, because they were quite in doubt whether the act was not perfectly legal!* Such a direction was so contrary to the direction given by the learned judges who have been quoted, that the passage is cited by way of contrast:—

"It may be that all I have said upon the subject of the law will leave you, as I candidly own it still leaves me, in some degree of doubt. Let me, therefore add, that if you are of opinion, on the whole, that the jurisdiction to exercise martial law is not satisfactorily made out, and that it is a matter which ought to be submitted to further consideration on the trial of the accused before a competent court, where all the questions of law may be raised and determined, I must say, I think the safer course will be to let the matter go forward" (p. 155).

It never seems to have occurred to the Lord Chief Justice that if he after a year or two to consider the law, still doubted about it, the act of the accused could not have been culpably illegal, still less feloniously malicious and murderous. Whether there was or was not any doubt upon the law he left to the grand jury, he was not in a position even to tell them that.

"If there was a power to put martial law in force, and consequently jurisdiction to try persons under it, that will be safely ascertained and firmly established by judicial decision. If there was none, it follows that there has been a miscarriage of justice which calls for public inquiry.

"If, however, upon a review of the authorities, you think the accused ought not to be further harassed by criminal proceedings, you will say so

---

* It is but fair to the Lord Chief Justice to say that he may have been aware that Lord Campbell and Lord Cottenham had given their sanction to a despatch in the Ceylon case, in which what may be called the *formal* legality of martial law was left in much confusion. The despatch was confidential, and has never been published, but, as Earl Grey has done the Author the honour of allowing him to copy it, the noble Earl may have shown it to the Lord Chief Justice, and it was certainly calculated to leave his mind in great doubt, for, as will be seen from a perusal of it (in the Author's Review of the Authorities), it is extremely confused. But surely the Lord Chief Justice should have given Mr. Eyre the benefit of the doubt.

by ignoring the bill. Upon this you must exercise your own judgment" (p. 155).

So that it will be manifest there was not, nor could there possibly be, in such a charge, any exposition of the law as to martial law, that is, no authentic judicial direction to which any judicial authority could possibly attach.

In a word the whole charge was mere argument, one half upon the law, the other half upon the facts, and there was no judicial direction, from beginning to end upon the subject of martial law, except that he could not say what the law was, and that he rather advised the grand jury to find bills for murder against the accused in order that the law might be settled.

In the case in which Mr. Justice Blackburn charged the grand jury the case was in every respect wholly different. There, in the first place, the case not only directly and necessarily involved the whole subject of martial law, but it raised every question of law which could possibly arise out of it. For the charge was not one of murder, and so not embarrassed with the question of felonious motive. It was a mere indictment for misdemeanour, in which any degree of grave culpability, whether in act or omission, whether gross recklessness or gross neglect, would support a conviction. And as it was the result of two years' consideration, aided by the enormous advantage of a previous inquiry before a Royal Commission, and the examination of the Governor upon oath, it embraced every charge which could by possibility be brought against a colonial Governor, or any other high officer, at home or abroad, connected with his conduct in the suppression of riot or rebellion, whether or not under martial law. There was every possible variety of charge, supported by every possible kind of evidence. There was the charge of illegally *declaring* martial law and illegally carrying it out at all, and the charge of continuing it too long, or allowing its *excessive* execution. There were cases of executions and cases of punishments under martial law; cases of arrest and imprisonment not under martial

c

law; cases of deaths inflicted on the field and of deaths inflicted by sentence of court-martial; cases in which it was not proved that the Governor knew or assented to anything; cases in which a knowledge was implied from his being in the neighbourhood, and assent was implied from means of knowledge; or cases in which actual assent was shown, as in the instance of the execution of Gordon, and the arrest of several other persons. So that the *general* question of the legality of martial law, and every special or particular question which could possibly arise under it, or with reference to the suppression of riot or rebellion, was directly raised in some or other of twenty different counts.

And then again, the learned judge rigidly confined himself to his own proper province or function, the declaration of matter of law, in the way of judicial direction to the grand jury; and, on the one hand, carefully abstained from travelling into any irrelevant questions of law, and, on the other hand, gave clear, plain, positive directions on such questions of law as *were* relevant; so that everything he said on the subject had judicial authority. Hence it is obvious that his charge, even if it stood entirely on its own merits, must be infinitely the more valuable and of greater authority; and if there were any inconsistency between his and that of the Lord Chief Justice, the *latter* must be discarded.

But it did *not* stand merely on its own merits; for whereas the Lord Chief Justice avowed that he had not had any opportunity of discussion with his brethren before delivering his charge, Mr. Justice Blackburn was able to state that he had had the immense advantage of the assistance of all his brethren, not merely the judges of his own Court but the others; so that there was every reason to believe that his view of the law had their general concurrence, and there never was an exposition of the law delivered with greater authority, at all events in such a form.

It is true that, as already mentioned, the Lord Chief

Justice made an attempt to disparage or diminish the authority of the charge, by controverting the extent to which he and the other judges of his Court had given their assent; but it will be found, upon close examination, that the result was only more fully to confirm the legal authority of the charge of Mr. Justice Blackburn, and to support the statement he had made. For as regarded the central proposition, the governing direction given to the grand jury as to the question for their consideration, and the *ratio decidendi* on which they were to determine the case, it appeared that it had been *reduced into writing*, and in that written form acknowledged and assented to by the Lord Chief Justice and his learned brethren; so that this, at all events—which was the most important part, the core and kernel of the whole—was the opinion of *a unanimous and united Court*. And it will be found, upon close examination, that all the rest, *so far as it is matter of law*, can logically be deduced or worked out from the premises or principles involved in that great central proposition.

And as to the difference of opinion on other points, as to the other judges, it merely came to this, that they were not prepared to assent, not that they could venture to dissent and to declare the law to be otherwise: so that their mere non-assent came to little or nothing; for it was manifest that, except one of them, Mr. Justice Hannen, they had not given the subject such attention, as that their inability to assent could, to any great extent, impair the authority of a clear, positive declaration of the law by a very able judge, who had, under a sense of judicial responsibility, given the whole question his most careful study and consideration. And the only point on which the Lord Chief Justice *dissented*, viz., as to the removal into the declared district, was not (as already shown) a proposition of *law* at all, and it was moreover utterly irrelevant and immaterial.

The charge of Mr. Justice Blackburn, therefore, had the very highest degree of judicial authority which it is possible to attach to any judicial declaration of the law, short of an absolute legal decision.

The learned judge very clearly laid down all the propositions of law as to martial law which were necessary for the direction of the jury upon all the various counts or charges in the indictment; whether as to what it is, or as to the legality of its declaration in time of rebellion, or as to the duty of the Governor with reference to its continuance, or the control of its execution. As regarded the first point—the legality of its declaration in time of rebellion—the learned judge, indeed, with characteristic caution (so anxious was he not to lay down a single proposition which it was not necessary to lay down—which, of course, only lends greater weight to those which he *did* lay down) sought, as far as possible, to ground himself upon the enactment of the Colonial Act, allowing martial law to be declared. But as this begins by reciting that it may be necessary to declare martial law, which of itself recognises and implies that there was a precedent power to declare martial law; and as it goes on, upon the one hand, to allow of it where it would not, as all admit, be allowed at common law; viz., in time not only of *actual*, but of *apprehended* rebellion: and upon the other hand, imposes an important condition or restriction upon its declaration, viz., that it shall only be by consent of the Council; and lastly as it does not define or explain martial law, but simply says there shall be power to declare martial law in the case and on the condition thus mentioned, it is manifest that it leaves the whole question open—*what martial law is;* and, moreover, plainly implies and assumes that there *was* such a thing as martial law known to the law of England before, because the common law had been, as to personal rights of *British born* subjects and their descendants, extended to the island. And hence on all hands it has been admitted that the question of what the statute meant must turn upon what martial law meant at common law, and that what it meant at common law, and in other statutes mentioning it, that it must mean in the Colonial Act. And the learned judge very clearly told the jury that it meant in effect the temporary establishment of military power in suspension of, and in substitution for, the ordinary law of the land, as in time of war, and that it included what the Petition of Right described as "the summary justice of martial law, that is, military executions of rebels by military tribunals. And as the learned judge very clearly pronounced his opinion that the martial law thus mentioned and defined in the Petition of Right *was not abolished* by it, it is manifest, he held, that by the common law martial law in time of rebellion is lawful. But, at all events, the learned judge clearly held that on an act allowing martial law to be declared by the advice of the Council, martial law might legally be declared and executed in the *sense in which the Council understood it*, and without any criminal liability; and that as they understood it in the sense of military rule, it might, without any criminal liability, be so declared and executed.

The same principle was carefully applied by the learned Judge to the question of the *continuance* of martial law: a question, it is obvious, substantially the same. For the learned Judge directed the grand jury that the Governor would not be criminally liable without grave culpability, and that this could not attach if there was an exercise of ordinary sense and firmness in an extraordinary emergency, and it is ordinary sense to act upon the best advice which was to be obtained. So that, if a governor, in continuing martial law, acted (as Mr. Eyre did) with the advice of those most competent to advise him, he could not be criminally liable, because not gravely culpable. This is in accordance with legal principle and common sense.

On the other hand, there is an entire consistency between the view taken by Mr. Justice Blackburn of the *culpability* or criminal responsibility of a governor for the conduct or continuance of measures of this kind, and the view which had already been taken by the highest and most eminent authorities, whether constitutional lawyers or constitutional statesmen. The general result of the learned judge's direction was undoubtedly understood to be for an acquittal; for it appeared to come, in substance, to this, that a man in a responsible position in a trying emergency could not be criminally liable, because not gravely culpable, who, in such an emergency, showed reasonable and ordinary sense and firmness; and that the practical test of this would be the aspect of affairs *at the time*, and his taking the best advice he could obtain. Such had been in substance the view laid down by former judges, whether as to colonial governors or magistrates in similar emergencies, that a man could not be culpable for acting on the best advice he could get, and forming the best opinion he could upon the circumstances as they appeared to him at the time. This was the view laid down by the Lord Chief Justice himself when Attorney-General in the Ceylon Case. For he said, having laid down that—

"When martial law is in force, the ordinary criminal tribunals cease to have jurisdiction;" . . . "in considering the question of punishment, it is necessary that *the Governor should look at all the surrounding circumstances of the case*. We do not punish men merely for the offence they have committed. They are punished in order to deter others from following their example. It is all very well to talk of a bloodless rebellion, suppressed without difficulty. But let us recollect the spirit of the people, their disaffection with Government, and *all the circumstances* connected with the native population of the colony." (Hansard's Debates, vol. 115, p. 227.)

This was the view laid down by an eminent statesman on the same occasion :—

"The news of the insurrection came suddenly upon the Governor. He immediately *sent for an officer in whose discretion and experience he might well trust, and he acted according to that opinion.* He immediately saw the general commanding the forces, he took means by which the rebellion might be promptly suppressed, and in order to do that more effectually with the concurrence of the General and the Attorney-General, he proclaimed martial law in the district which was disturbed." (Lord Russell, debate on Ceylon, House of Commons, May, 1851.)

This view was, it should be observed, laid down as well of the *continuance* as of the original declaration of martial law; and it came, in a word, to this, that a governor was not even censurable, much less gravely culpable, who, upon such questions, *acted on the best advice he could obtain.*

"The Governor, in this matter, acted in concert with and with the advice of his Executive Council ; and, finding that there was a preponderance of opinion in the Council in favour of continuing martial law, and that, above all, the General commanding the district was strenuous in advising that the operation of martial law should be continued—he continued it. The Governor was *guided by opinions which he had conscientiously formed ; supported, as he was, by those who ought to advise him in the colony.* And we ought not to throw any censure upon him on questions upon which, if there could be any difference of opinion, he was *more likely to judge rightly from the circumstances before him, with the assistance of his advisers.*" (Ibid.)

It is obvious that, in the view of this eminent statesman, reasonable and ordinary judgment, as well as honesty, were shown by taking and acting on the best and most competent advice that could be obtained. And it would be impossible to conceive a better test of *ordinary* judgment than the opinion of the most competent persons ; nor could there be a better guide to what is reasonable on such a question than the opinion of an experienced statesman, seeing that culpability is not a question, as the learned Judge observed, of exact definition, but one necessarily of measure, opinion, and degree. Hence, the scope of the learned judge's direction, on the question of culpability, or the acts for which the Governor was responsible, were in accordance with these views.

So it was in entire accordance with the view taken by the Commissioners, *up to a certain point,* as to the declaration and continuance of martial law, in full operation, for a considerable part—about half—of the whole period. For they reported—

"With the full knowledge of all that has occurred, we are, nevertheless, also of opinion that, *with the information before them,* and with the knowledge they possessed of the state and circumstances of the island, the Council of War had good reason for the advice which they gave, and that the Governor was well *justified in acting upon that advice."*

So that the Commissioners put the propriety of the Governor's conduct on his acting on information and *advice.* When, indeed, they came to consider the *continuance* of martial law for the full period, they lose sight of this altogether, and no longer allow the Governor the merit of acting properly, although they admit that he *continued to act upon information and advice.* There is a manifest inconsistency here, and few will refuse to admit that the eminent statesman above quoted, and the learned judge, were far more consistent in applying the same test, and allowing the benefit of it to the same extent during the *whole* period of the duration of martial law; for why should a Governor, at a certain point, all of a sudden, believe his advisers wrong? And if he had done so, and disregarded their advice, and the rebellion had broken out again, where would have been his excuse?

The Commissioners fully recognised the *principle* laid down by the learned judge, that matters must be looked at as they *appeared at the time* :—

"*We know how much easier it is to decide this question after than before the event,* and we are aware, too, that sometimes the success of the measures adopted for the prevention of an evil, deprives the authors of these measures of the evidence they would otherwise have had of their necessity. *We have endeavoured, therefore, to place ourselves, as far as is possible, in the position of the Governor and his advisers, at the time their determination was arrived at.* The only thing to be feared was simultaneous risings in other parts of the island. The question to be considered, in deciding upon the conduct of the Government, *is not whether such risings were in fact likely to take place,* but whether the Government, with the information then in their hands, had *reasonable grounds for apprehending they might take place.* It will be seen that they were receiving almost daily reports from different parts of the island, which must have led them to the conclusion that considerable danger of such risings existed. They could not at the time investigate, as we have, the grounds on which those reports rested. They were forwarded by the custodes of different parishes, in whom the Government was bound to place a certain amount of confidence, and they *would have incurred a serious responsibility if they had,* with this in-

formation, thrown away the advantage of the terror inspired by the name of martial law." (Report.)

Only they thought the trial ought to have been stopped earlier. They, however, arbitrarily stopped short in the application of their principle, that acting upon competent evidence takes away culpability; but the learned judge adhered to it consistently throughout. And, as to this, the Commissioners reported—

"That by the continuance of martial law in its full force, to the extreme limit of its statutory operation, the people were deprived, for a longer than necessary period of the great constitutional privileges by which the security of life and property is provided for."

But then they also reported, in effect, that this had not been of much practical injury, for they stated in effect that the sentences of the courts-martial were almost always just.

"In the great majority of cases the evidence seems to have been unobjectionable in character, and quite sufficient to justify the findings of the court."

And they only mention three cases in which the evidence was insufficient in amount, so that their general statements of excessive punishments and too frequent executions could scarcely have referred, at all events largely, to the courts-martial. These general statements no doubt referred to the rash and hasty inflictions of death during the first excitement, and most of them by soldiers without orders, and here the Commissioners were very careful to *discriminate the responsibilities of different parties*, and not to throw the blame upon the officers of acts of the soldiers, without orders or in their absence, nor upon the commander, of the fault of officers, nor upon the Governor of the non-control of matters purely military. Thus, when mentioning wanton acts of soldiers they do not blame the officers, nor when lamenting the absence of proper instructions to the officers, do they blame the

Governor, they being well aware that it was not for him, but the Commander-in-chief to issue instructions to military officers. It should seem that the Secretary of State must have taken a different view, for one of the grounds on which he censured and recalled the Governor was the absence of precise instructions to the officers. It appears that the learned judge took the same view as the Commissioners, for he did not say a word to imply any such duty to the Governor, although the whole scheme and theory of the prosecution evidently assumed that the Governor was responsible for whatever was done by anybody during martial law. The learned judge on the other hand told the jury distinctly that the Governor was not responsible for acts done by soldiers with or without orders of officers, unless there was evidence of some authority or sanction on the part of the Governor, nor was he liable for the absence of directions to the officers, which it was for the military commander to issue.

On the same general principle upon which lawyers and statesmen were thus united, in holding that a Governor who, with the advice of his council, carried out martial law could not be gravely culpable either for its declaration or continuance, because he could not be deemed to have acted without ordinary sense and judgment, it would follow that he could not be gravely culpable for committing the execution of martial law to military authority. And this was the spirit and principle of the direction of the learned judge as to the responsibility of the Governor, for the control of martial law, whether as to its exercise in the field, or as to the execution of military prisoners tried by courts-martial. As to the former, there was some evidence of some instances of excess, but the learned judge told the grand jury, in plain and distinct terms, that as there was no evidence that Mr. Eyre knew of or had authorized them, therefore he was not responsible for them; a direction in accordance with plain principles of law, and in which the *whole court concurred*, and there is every reason to believe (from what the learned judge said) *all the judges*. And it was clearly conveyed to the grand jury and may be taken as clear law, that on such an occasion the Governor is only liable for orders he himself gives, or at all events knows of and allows, or for acts he authorizes or directs; and that he is not responsible merely because he did not issue orders to the military officers, which there is no reason to believe he has legal power to give, to *prevent* excesses which he had no reason to anticipate.

In the next place as to the military executions under orders of court-martial, the evidence not going beyond a general knowledge by the Governor that such executions were going on, and also disclosing that they were executions *after trial*, the learned judge was not called upon to give more than a general direction, which was in substance this: that the rules of regular trials or of ordinary law did not apply, but that it was enough if there was an honest inquiry and an honest endeavour to get at the truth; in a word, the substance, without the mere forms or formalities of justice, a direction entirely in accordance with the previous judicial decisions upon the subject,* and with sound sense and legal principle.

It was a direction also entirely in accordance with the opinion of the Royal Commissioners, including the Recorder, one of the ablest judges in the country, aided by Mr. Maule, one of our soundest lawyers, confirmed and followed by the official opinion of the law officers of the Crown, including that accomplished jurist and constitutional lawyer, Sir Roundel Palmer; that very able and experienced Crown lawyer, Sir R. Collier; and that most learned and most eminent lawyer, Mr. Hannen, now Mr. Justice Hannen. The Report of the Commissioners, which, on the advice of these great lawyers, the Government approved, stated—

"The number of executions by order of courts-martial appeared to us

---

* See Wall's Case, 28 State Trials, and Wright *v.* Fitzgerald, 27 State Trials, and Rex *v.* Suddis, East's Reports.

so large, that it became very important to ascertain, as far as we are able, the *principles* upon which the members constituting the courts acted, and the sort of evidence upon which their decisions were pronounced. *It would be unreasonable to expect that in the circumstances under which these courts were assembled, there should be the same perfect regularity and adherence to technical rules which we are accustomed to witness in our ordinary tribunals; but there are certain great principles which ought under no circumstances to be violated,* and there is an amount of evidence which every tribunal should require before it pronounces a judgment which shall affect the life, liberty, or person of any human being. In order to ascertain whether these principles have been adhered to, and whether in all cases this necessary evidence has been required, we have carefully read the notes of the evidence given before the different courts, upon which notes the confirmations of the sentences were pronounced. *In the great majority of the cases the evidence seems to have been unobjectionable in character, and quite sufficient to justify the finding of the court."*

The sound sense of this view surely must be manifest to every one, lawyer or layman; and it is in accordance with the views of our most enlightened writers, such as Jeremy Bentham* and Mill.†

The above is the view which the writer had endeavoured to convey, and which he certainly in many passages *had most clearly conveyed*, in his "Treatise on Martial Law;" but there were other passages which he supposes were not so accurately written as they ought to have been, in which the Lord Chief Justice imagined it was meant that men ought to be convicted on evidence not substantially sufficient. Nothing was further from the writer's intention.

The *importance* of the above view with reference to the trials by court-martial, and especially to the case of Gordon, will be equally obvious. In treating of the latter case, however, in the case of Colonel Nelson, who had approved of the finding, the Lord Chief Justice adopted an entirely different view, and entirely departed from the judicial decisions in the cases of Governor Wall and *Wright* v. *Fitzgerald*, and though he never ventured distinctly to lay down that there must be an observance of the rules of

---

* See Bentham's Rationale of Judicial Evidence, vol. iv.
† See Mill's History of British India, vol. v.

regular or ordinary tribunals, he conveyed to the jury that impression, for he commented upon every piece of evidence adduced in Gordon's case, with reference to those rules, in their strictest form, and indeed, in his endeavours to impeach the evidence in that case, he went far beyond the law, even as to the rules of regular and ordinary tribunals. And it is manifest that the Lord Chief Justice would not be satisfied with the above, and enforced the strict rules of law. By commenting upon the evidence in that way, although trying, *not Gordon, but the men who tried him*, the Lord Chief Justice conveyed to the jury the notion that even by ordinary law a criminal conviction can be impeached by showing that there was a non-observance of regular rules, or that evidence was received which was legally inadmissible. Yet no one knows better than he that this is not so. For in Winsor's case, the evidence of a fellow prisoner— accused of the same crime, and not only *liable* to trial, but under trial—was received, contrary to all practice, without first taking an acquittal; and all the judges of England—headed by the Lord Chief Justice—declared most truly not only that by our law no writ of error lay for it, but that there was no reason for staying execution, because it appeared that the *prisoner had sustained no substantial injustice*. And yet he made it a great point against the conviction in Gordon's case, and one or two others, that a witness was himself a rebel, and *therefore liable to be tried!* The very point he himself had overruled in Winsor's case! Nor is this all. He actually, in the strongest terms, denounced the conviction in Gordon's case, because, after taking the strictly legal evidence of the witnesses sworn and examined and cross-examined in the ordinary way, the President read their depositions, to check or confirm them! Here again, not only had this been declared perfectly legal, even in a regular court-martial, in a great case* which the Lord Chief Justice himself cited for another

---

* Grant *v.* Gould, 2 Henry Blackstone's Reports.

purpose (though he neither mentioned that nor any other of the judicial decisions on the point), but it is the *constant practice in our criminal courts*, and one which is so reasonable and so conducive to justice that just before these trials took place Parliament had passed an Act to facilitate it, and remove every technical difficulty which lay in its way, where the deposition had *not* been taken in the presence of the person, as is really necessary when the deposition is to be used *in the absence* of the witness, and to *dispense* with his oral evidence. For that Act—known as Mr. Denman's—provides

"That a witness may be cross-examined as to previous statements made by him in writing or *reduced into writing* relative to the subject matter of the indictment, . . . provided that it shall be *competent for the Judge at any time during the trial to require the production of the writing for his inspection, and he may thereupon make such use of it for the purposes of the trial as he may think fit.*" (27 & 28 Vict., c. 18, s. 5, Act for Amending the Law of Evidence and Practice on Criminal Trials, 9th May, 1865.)

Here, therefore, Parliament had expressly provided that at any time during a trial the Judge might call for a former statement of the witness, and read it, and the Lord Chief Justice, in his charge, delivered some time after that Act had been in operation, denounced it as "one of the most lamentable departures from every principle of procedure that could well be imagined!" (Charge, p. 132.) It is well known to be most conducive to justice, as it often happens that a witness varies from his evidence, one way or the other. In this case, however, in the most important instance, he did *not;* so that, in any view, there was no substantial injustice or injury. And even as to his comments on the use of depositions in the *absence* of the witness (which our law allows, if they have been taken in the prisoner's presence), although, no doubt, this is not advisable, in any case, nor proper, where the depositions are the *sole* evidence : the Lord Chief Justice entirely forgot that he was not trying Gordon, nor even reviewing his case in a Court of Appeal, but *trying those who tried him ;* and that, therefore, the only question was *substantial injustice or injury,* as to which he entirely omitted to remind the jury that these depositions were *not* the sole, nor even the principal evidence, but that the principal evidence was strictly legal ; and he surely ought to have mentioned that there was *no substantial injustice shown,* especially as, in fact, there had not been any ; for it was notorious that the chief witnesses, whose depositions had been read, had been strictly cross-examined before the Commissioners, and adhered to their evidence. And if the Lord Chief Justice was right in his view that the *whole* evidence was insufficient (which he took an hour or two to argue), of what use was it to consider the legal admissibility of this or that piece of evidence ? On the other hand, *as the effect was for the jury,* he had no right to express any opinion upon it, and was bound to assume that they might think it sufficient, or even the *legal* evidence ; and then there would be no substantial injustice, *even if the evidence was shown to be false,* as to which there was not any evidence, and it was to be assumed to be true. Happily, therefore, the observations of the Lord Chief Justice on the point were of no judicial authority, seeing that they were entirely irrelevant to the issue, and departed from the opinion of all the judges in Winsor's case, that the real test, *even* in a trial by ordinary law, is *not* regularity, but substantial justice. On the other hand, the ruling of Mr. Justice Blackburn is in accordance with all the authorities, and was strictly relevant, the charge not being murder, but misdemeanour for allowing improper trials ; and therefore it is of judicial authority.

Upon the principles thus laid down by Mr. Justice Blackburn, it would follow, of course, that the Governor, while he would be liable for illegal acts personally directed by himself, as acts of arrest, would not be liable for injuries not actually nor legally consequent upon his own acts. Thus, in regard to several arrests he was proved to have ordered out of the declared district, and removals into that district; it appearing that in one of these cases, Gordon's, death was inflicted by the military authorities under sentence of court-martial, and in another case (that of one Phillip) flogging in like manner was inflicted; there being no evidence that these acts were done by Mr. Eyre's orders or authority, although, as to the former mentioned case he declared his approval, nothing was said by the learned judge to imply that the Governor was responsible for these subsequent acts as legally consequent upon his own. He would be responsible, therefore, for the arrest and removal into the declared district, but not for the trial by court-martial, or the infliction of the sentence, whether flogging or hanging, as the case might be. For these would not be in a legal sense consequences of the removal into the district; since the liability to trial by court-martial, assuming martial law to be legal, would not follow from the person being within the district, but from having caused or committed an offence there. And the removal would not be the actual cause of the trials, unless they took place under the authority or by the directions of the Governor, which did not appear, and was not the fact, as they took place under military authority. And again, assuming martial law to be illegal, the trials could still less be the consequences, in a legal sense, of the removal, for if there were no such thing as martial law, then the removal could make no difference, and if those who tried the parties did so under the military authority, only military authorities would be liable.

It has been already observed, that the Lord Chief Justice had no right nor legal power to pronounce any opinion upon the legality of the removal into a declared district, for in the case before him, that of the military commander and officer, who had nothing to do with the removal, the question did not arise, and he, himself, said that it could not affect the legality of the trial, for which alone they were responsible; so that his observations upon that point were utterly irrelevant and extra-judicial.

But in the case before Mr. Justice Blackburn, the point distinctly arose, for the case was that of the Governor who ordered the removal; and there was a distinct count for the removal. His direction, therefore, on the point had judicial authority. And to a great extent, to the full extent to which it was important, his direction was agreed to by all the judges.

All the judges appeared to have agreed that the assumed illegality of an arrest and removal into the declared district would not render a subsequent trial and sentence there illegal. And the learned judge laid it down distinctly that it might be lawful under proper circumstances to remove a person into the declared district to be tried there by court-martial. As to the circumstances which would be proper, he applied the same test as in other matters, reasonable and honest belief of necessity. The application of this test he left to the grand jury as a question of fact. The Lord Chief Justice seemed to think it not a question of law (for he laid down no general rule or principle), but a question of *fact* for *him* to determine: for he declared that the removal of, *Gordon* was unlawful and unjustifiable. It is conceived that Mr. Justice Blackburn was clearly right, according to the authorities, according to legal principle, according to good sense, and according to necessity, which lies at the base of the whole question. For it seems scarcely possible to contend that if the trial and execution of the author of a rebellion appears to be necessary for its suppression, he cannot be touched, if he takes care to keep out of the district, except through the slow and doubtful processes of common law. Besides, as the whole colony may be declared, the point is purely technical, for it merely arises on the *proclamation* of martial law. The truth is, however, that in such a case, there is no exercise of martial law until the trial takes place, and *that* cannot take place by martial law out of the district, and when it takes place, it is by reason, not of the arrest and removal, but by reason of acts done or caused within the district.

Next, the learned judge laid it down that a Governor is not liable for acts which he does not direct nor authorise, *and there was no evidence that Mr. Eyre had directed or authorised the trial of Gordon upon evidence which was insufficient;* and, on the contrary, as the evidence in Colonel Nelson's case, before the Lord Chief Justice, showed, and the undoubted *fact* was, that he only desired that the man should be tried *if there was sufficient evidence*, and if it was proper that he should be tried. (Evidence of Colonel Nelson, Minutes of Evidence, pp. 622—625, which was included in the evidence in Colonel Nelson's case.) That he referred to the military commander, and there was no evidence that he had allowed or approved the execution knowing the evidence was insufficient; but on the contrary it would rather appear that, as the trial took place under military authority, and as according to the well-known course of military usage, it was for the military commander to review the evidence, he would naturally *assume* that the evidence was sufficient, and would merely consider whether, *assuming* guilt, there was any reason why the sentence should not be executed. It would follow, that even supposing the evidence to have been insufficient, there was no ground for imputing, merely on that account, any grave culpability to the Governor, in this or any other case by trial by court-martial. And the only question would be, whether he allowed the execution under an honest belief in its necessity for the suppression of the *rebellion*. Not the mere outbreak, but the *rebellion*, of which the massacre and insurrection were only the outbreak. A question which would depend upon all the circumstances of the colony, and the aspect of affairs at the time.

This principle would apply to all the trials by court-martial, in the absence of any evidence, that the evidence was brought to the consideration of the Governor before its conviction, or that he authorised convictions in the absence of sufficient evidence. And it would apply to the number of those executed or punished, as well as to the nature of the cases in which the executions or punishments took place; two questions closely connected; for if the Governor might fairly presume that the evidence was sufficient, he might fairly presume that the sentences were just, and so in neither view could he be responsible for excesses, in whatever sense the words might be used, unless it could be shown that he authorised or *knowingly* allowed unjust convictions or sentences, of which there was no evidence.

It is most remarkable that, although the charge most pressed against the Governor was that of Gordon, on account of the vulgar error that his removal into the declared district was an exercise of martial law *out* of the district, and that because he had not taken an *active* part in the insurrection, and had kept personally out of it therefore he was not liable to be dealt with under martial law; yet the law officers of the Crown, in effect, advised that his trial and execution were legal, as they advised that *all acts done by military authority within the declared district were legal;* and, upon the evidence, the *trial and execution* clearly were by military authority, and the Lord Chief Justice admitted that the alleged illegality of the arrest would be immaterial. And it is still more remarkable that, in effect, the Lord Chief Justice himself virtually admitted the entire legality of Gordon's arrest and trial, assuming, what seems now to be established, that either at common law or by statute, martial law, in any sense, is allowable in rebellion. This, indeed, he entirely admits, for he himself argued throughout his charge that martial law, as to rebels, means the same thing as military law as to soldiers. This view must rest upon the assumption (for which there is strong foundation in constitutional law) that the command of all bodies of armed men belongs to the Crown, since the Mutiny Act and

Articles of War only apply to armed men under the command of the Crown. Taking that view, however—*the view of the Lord Chief Justice*—it would follow that the *arrest, removal, and trial of Gordon were perfectly legal and regular.* For, as to the arrest and removal, as already stated, it was held by the twelve judges after the Revolution that a soldier could be sent, even in time of peace, from this country to Ireland to be tried by martial law there during a war or rebellion. And next, the Mutiny Act and Articles of War make sedition capital as to all persons subject thereto. Then, as the Commissioners show, the substance of the charge was that Gordon had incited the insurgents to rebellion; and they also, in effect, state that Gordon did, in fact, excite, incite to, and cause the insurrection. The Lord Chief Justice propounded no other view or theory of martial law, than regular military law. And by the Mutiny Act, s. 15 declares—

"That if any person subject to the Act shall begin, excite, cause, or join in any meeting or sedition in any forces belonging to Her Majesty' army, or shall not use his utmost endeavours to suppress the same, &c., he shall suffer death."

The framers of the Mutiny Act evidently held the doctrine of the common law, that if a man excited to an insurrection he must be taken to have meant it, since he must have used language calculated to cause it.

The Lord Chief Justice quite agreed with the Commissioners, and said in his charge :—

"There cannot be the least doubt that an opinion was universally prevalent in the island that it was through Mr. Gordon's instrumentality, through his speeches and writings, and the *systematic agitation he had for some time been keeping up, that the mutinous and rebellious spirit had been engendered which broke out at last with this unhappy insurrection.* It may be that while *it suited his purpose to keep the passions of the black population in a state of ferment bordering upon outbreak,* he persuaded himself he could keep them under subjection. That this system of agitation, working upon the minds of an ignorant, unenlightened population, capable of sudden outbreaks of passion, and which it then became impossible to control, did produce a state of excited feeling which, when the torch was applied to the train, exploded in this terrible calamity there can be no doubt. (Charge, p. 151.)

And though the Lord Chief Justice still would have it that there was no evidence that Gordon intended "this insurrection"—*this* insurrection, observe—it is manifest that he was not aware that he had, according to the well-established doctrine of our law, already, in the above passage stated abundant evidence; for no one could suppose that Gordon was the only man who did not understand the natural effect of his own language, or that he did not understand the black population. So that it merely comes to this, that he did not *intend the outbreak on the particular occasion*. Very likely not; it was most providentially precipitated. But in law he was not less liable for it. And the Lord Chief Justice forgot his own argument that martial law is military law, under which, beyond all doubt, by his own showing, Gordon was rightly executed. By military law, as has been seen, it is a capital offence to excite men to insurrection. The Commissioners and the Lord Chief Justice concurred in saying that Gordon *did* excite men to insurrection. The court-martial which tried him was constituted (although the Lord Chief Justice by mistake thought otherwise) strictly according to the provisions of the Mutiny Act; and the Lord Chief Justice himself says that they believed the man guilty of the offence with which he was charged and indeed himself states, in effect, that the man was guilty. It follows that upon the view of the Lord Chief Justice, Gordon was rightly executed, and that the view taken by the late law officers of the Crown, in making no exception in that case as to the legality of the trials, was correct.

At all events the effect of the ruling of Mr. Justice Blackburn was, that no grave culpability attached to the Governor in respect of that or any other case. The learned judge declared the removal would be legal under proper circumstances, and the grand jury found that they *were* proper, or, at all events, that the Governor might not unreasonably believe so. And the dissent of the Lord Chief Justice upon the point is immaterial, for it was wholly extra-judicial, and of no judicial authority, being a question for the grand jury. Indeed, the observations of the Lord Chief Justice went upon a misapprehension in supposing that the learned judge had laid down that the removal was justifiable. The learned judge laid down the law to be that the removal would not be gravely culpable if honestly and reasonably ordered; and the grand jury found that it was so. And the learned judge distinctly told the grand jury that the Governor was not liable for executions he had not authorised or knowingly allowed. The direction, on the whole, amounted to a direction to ignore the bill, which they accordingly did.

Thus, then, the direction of the learned Judge and the finding of the grand jury amounted to an acquittal of Mr. Eyre, as to any grave culpability upon any of the matters charged against him, embracing all those upon which he was condemned, and others also.

With regard to the *continuance* of martial law, it is very remarkable that it appears to have escaped the attention of the Royal Commissioners, of the Secretary of State, and of the Lord Chief Justice, that the very object of the Colonial Act was to allow of the continuance of martial law during the continuance of *danger*. As in the Imperial Act, 43 Geo. III., c. 117, as to Ireland, passed the very next year after the Colonial Governors Act, and which expressly allowed and declared to be expedient, the *execution* of martial law for a considerable period after the suppression of *open* rebellion, and as to persons *not* taken in open rebellion, and as to all persons aiding and abetting it. But the learned judge carefully pointed out the immense difference which the Colonial Act made in this respect, as to the continuance of the martial law in force. The Local Act contained nothing to suggest that martial law, while maintained, was not to be enforced; and the learned judge left the question, as one of honesty and reasonableness, to the jury. The Imperial Act alluded to strongly indicates the view of the Legislature that it may be reasonable to keep martial law *in force* after actual rebellion has ceased, so long as *danger* exists. For that act expressly proved that it should be in force for six weeks after the next session; and that martial law might be exercised, whether or not the ordinary courts should be open; and for the punishment of all persons aiding the rebellion.

It may be convenient here to insert the Colonial Governors Act on which the prosecution proceeded. The 42 Geo. III., c. 85, recites :—

"That persons holding and exercising public employment out of Great Britain often escape punishment for offences committed by them, for want of courts having sufficient jurisdiction, by reason of their departing from the country where such offences have been committed, and that such persons cannot be tried in Great Britain for such offences as the law now stands (*i.e.*, except under the prior Act which applied only to Governors and military Commanders), and enacted, that if any person who shall hold or exercise any public station or office out of Great Britain shall commit or be guilty of any crime, misdemeanour, or offence, in the execution, or under colour, or in the exercise of such station or office, every such crime, misdemeanour, or offence, may be prosecuted in the court of King's Bench in England, either upon an information exhibited by the Attorney-General, or upon an indictment found, in which the crime, offence, or misdemeanour may be laid or charged to have been committed in Middlesex, and all such persons shall, on conviction, be liable to such punishment as may, by any laws now in force or Acts that may be passed, be inflicted for *any such crime, misdemeanour, or offence*, committed in England, and shall also be liable, at the discretion of the court of King's Bench, to be adjudged to be incapable of serving the Crown in any other office or station, civil or military."

No case had previously arisen under the statute except two, in both of which the proceedings proved abortive: one,* because the charge was felony, and the other, that of General Picton,† because the Court considered the

---

* R. *v.* Shaw; 5 Maude & Selwyn Reports.
† In the State Trials.

verdict wrong by reason of the jury not having been directed to consider the *Local Laws*.

It has been considered proper to give the *evidence*, and it has been given as it was returned by the magistrate to the Court.

The learned Judge has kindly revised the *text of his charge*, (which was sent to him, from the shorthand writer's notes,) but it need hardly be added that he is *responsible for nothing else.*

TEMPLE,

18*th July*, 1868.

REPORT OF THE CASE

OF

THE QUEEN

v.

EDWARD JOHN EYRE, ESQ.,

IN THE COURT OF QUEEN'S BENCH.

I.—THE EVIDENCE.*

The examination of John Dunning and others, taken on oath this 15th day of May, 1868, at the Police-court, Bow Street, in the County of Middlesex, and within the Metropolitan Police District, before me, the undersigned, one of the magistrates of the police-courts of the metropolis, sitting at the police-court aforesaid, in the presence and hearing of Edward John Eyre, who was charged this day before me.

This deponent, John Dunning, on his oath saith :—

I am a short-hand writer, and was present at the sittings of the Jamaica Commission. I produce the original notes made by me of the examination of Governor Eyre. The printed transcript of the notes is correct, with the written corrections.

(The printed transcript read.)

James Drover Barnett, on his oath, saith :—

I am a short-hand writer; on 31st January, 1866, I took the further notes of the examination of Governor Eyre, and I now produce these notes. The printed transcript of the notes, with the written corrections, is correct.

.(Printed transcript read.)

---

* From the depositions returned by the Magistrate, Mr. Vaughan.

James Pread, on his oath, saith :—

I am clerk to Mr. Avory, Clerk of the Central Criminal Court. I produce a copy of proclamation of martial law in Jamaica, and a copy of proclamation of Charles II. (extending the common law to English-born subjects).

William Shaen, on his oath, saith :—

I am a solicitor at 8, Bedford-row. The copy of proclamation of Charles II., produced by the witness Pread, is an examined and correct copy of the proclamation in the Public Record Office, I examined it myself. The copy proclamation is now read.

John Gorrie, on his oath, saith :—

I have been called to the Jamaica Bar. The volumes before me are Jamaica Statutes. The first is 33rd Charles II. to the present reign. The last session of 1865 is not here.

Cross-examined :—

The district of Morant Bay is not in the same jurisdiction as Kingston. There are circuit courts sitting at Morant Bay. In the ordinary course offences committed in Kingston would be tried in the circuit court of the district.

Augustus Walter Hewit Lake, on his oath, saith :—

I was in the employment of the *Colonial Standard* newspaper, published at Kingston, Jamaica, and I lived in Kingston, and was there in October, 1865. On the 13th of that month I went to Morant Bay in the French steamer, "Caravelle." Governor Eyre, General Nelson also went. We reached Morant Bay at 7 in the evening, and Mr. Eyre landed. I saw several printed copies of the proclamation produced posted there, and they continued posted till I left on the 2nd November, 1865. I saw Mr. Eyre on shore the night we landed, and on one or two subsequent occasions, in the main street; he was stopped, and some communication was made to him in respect of a prisoner. I was present, close by. It was reported that a man lying ill wished to make some confession, and it was ordered that Mr. Marshalleck and another magistrate should attend and take his deposition. Afterwards I saw Mr. Eyre in the town; several officers and soldiers were there at the time. During the time I was there a great many prisoners were tried by court-martial. One court-martial was composed of Lieutenants H. Errington and Brand, and Ensign Kelly; more than a dozen persons were tried by that court-martial; over fifty persons were tried by that court; considerably more than fifty persons were executed. There were other courts-martial; the first that sat at Morant Bay was composed of Colonel Hunt, the Attorney-General, and three or four others. I recollect a third, composed of Colonels Hutchens, Lewis, and Spent, all of the Militia. Mr. Gordon was tried by the first court-martial I've mentioned. I saw his execution. A great many persons were flogged. I saw one man executed, without any trial, by the orders of the Provost-marshal; I heard the orders given. The man was ordered to receive fifty lashes, and on the forty-seventh lash his back was bleeding profusely; he turned round and groaned; the Provost-marshal ordered him to be taken from the gun; he was thrown on the broad of his back, a rope was put round his neck, and he was hoisted over a rail, like a barrel of flour, and a huge white stone placed between his arms, and his legs pulled down, stretched. This was between 18th October and 2nd November. During all that time there was no outbreak or disturbance of any kind. More than one woman was executed; one was named Sarah Francis; she was condemned by the first court-martial a day or two after we arrived at Morant Bay; I was present at that court-martial; I heard the sentence. I returned to Kingston on 2nd November. I know Dr. Bruce intimately, he was one of the prisoners at Morant Bay when I was there; I left him there a prisoner; he was not brought to trial during the time I was there; I saw him on one or two occasions at his window. No charge was preferred against him whilst I was there, that is, he was never brought before a court-martial. Dr. Bruce is a medical man, and coroner of Vere—a white man, and fully 70 years of age. He was brought to Morant Bay; he resided at Vere, which is about 70 miles from Morant Bay, and a good way the other side Kingston, and also over 70 miles from the nearest point of the proclaimed district. I know Mr. Levine, he was proprietor and editor of the *County Union* newspaper, his residence was at Montego Bay, about 160 miles from the nearest point of the proclaimed district. I saw him also in custody, he was brought to Morant Bay and I left him there. He was never brought before a court-martial whilst I was there. I was there to report for the paper; I was employed upon all that went on. Mr. Levine was a white man. I knew George William Gordon, I saw him brought to Morant Bay, he came on the steamer Wolverine, I saw him on board, he landed, I saw him land, Mr. Eyre was on board at the same time, so I saw them both there. When I returned to Kingston and when I left the ordinary tribunals were sitting.

Cross-examined :—

I am clerk to Messrs. Shaen and Roscoe, attorneys for this prosecution, and have been so for about fourteen months. I was examined before the Royal Commissioners more than once. The man was hanged (named Marshall) about 18th October. I did not see Mr. Eyre at that time at Morant Bay, I believe he was not there. During the time I was at Morant Bay none of the ordinary courts were sitting. I remained in the town of Morant Bay during my stay, it was then occupied by the military and the sailors. I first saw Dr. Bruce in the ctousdy of the police in Morant Bay, I did not see him brought there. I first saw Levine in the same way, and know in the same way how he came there. I had repeatedly been to Morant Bay, four years before. I saw the ruins of the Court-house that had been burnt down and it seemed recently done. Levine, Phillips, and Dr. Bruce were tried at a special commission at Kingston long after martial-law had been raised. *Levine was convicted, Bruce and Phillips were acquitted, bills were found against them.*

I decline to say whether actions have been brought by Dr. Bruce an Phillips, because I don't think I should divulge the secrets of my employers—I mean *I decline to answer any questions with reference to actions brought by my employers.*

Re-examined :—

Levine, Bruce, and Phillips were tried in the next year, in the first quarter. I cannot fix the date. There was an appeal against Levine's conviction. The appeal was dismissed and Levine released after undergoing six months' imprisonment. He had been pardoned.

By the Court:—

Mr. Levine's paper was published in Montego Bay. Levine, Bruce, and Phillips were not kept in custody till they were tried by the Special Commission. They were free. The first court-martial was being held whilst Mr. Eyre was at Morant Bay. Subsequently there were two courts-martial sitting at one time. Mr. Eyre was at Morant Bay when the first five executions took place. I don't mean on the ground. I was present when Dr. Bruce was released. He was brought from Morant Bay to Spanish Town in custody of a police serjeant, and released by the Chief Justice on bail to answer any indictment that may be preferred against him. That was ten to fourteen days after I left Morant Bay.

The examination of Augustus Walter Hewit Lake and others taken on oath this 19th day of May, 1868, at the Police-court, Bow Street, in the County of Middlesex, and within the Metropolitan Police District, before me, the undersigned, one of the magistrates of the police-courts of the metropolis, sitting at the police-court aforesaid, in the presence and hearing of Edward John Eyre, who was charged this day before me.

This deponent, Augustus Walter Hewit Lake, on his oath further saith as follows:—

I now produce the notes I took at the time, 14th October, 1865.

"The first day I saw any flogging was the 18th October. Thirty-three persons were flogged that day. They were not tried before they were flogged. Marshall was flogged on the 18th. On the 19th twelve persons were flogged. They had been tried by court-martial. On the 20th eight were flogged. On the 21st four were flogged, they had fifty lashes each. On the 23rd sixteen were flogged; on the 24th, four ; on the 25th, eight ; on the 26th, five ; and another batch, eighteen, on the same date ; on the

27th, four; on the 28th, two; and on that day I fell sick. I saw the first execution on the 14th October. Three men and one woman were then executed. I was present at the court-martial. The sentence was accompanied by a recommendation to mercy. I have a note made at the time. Mr. Eyre was at Morant Bay then. The woman was hanged. On the 18th I saw one man executed. On the 21st I saw twenty men executed. They had been tried. On the 23rd, eighteen men were hanged, and another, James Gordon, making nineteen. Mr. George William Gordon was one of those. On the 24th, sixteen men were hanged; on the 26th, sixteen men were hanged; on the 27th, eighteen were hanged, fifteen men and three women. On the 28th, eleven men were hanged."

Cross-examined :—

I now read my entry on the 14th October. It is as follows :—
"Three men and one woman hanged': Lewis Stuart, James Williams, Charles Pilid, Sarah Francis. Woman recommended to be commuted." I have no recollection of the ground mentioned for the recommendation. I have frequently seen Dr. Bruce at my employer's office during the fourteen months I have been there.

By the Court :—

I landed on the 13th October, and then order and tranquillity were restored at Morant Bay, and there was no subsequent outbreak whilst I was there. The last time I saw Mr. Eyre was on the 20th October, and one day between the 14th and the 20th, I believe he was away during the interval.

In reply to defendant's Counsel :—

I was not out of the town of Morant Bay during the time stated, and the town was then in the occupation of the naval and military powers.

By the Court :—

There are little villages three or four miles from Morant Bay which are called the district of Morant Bay.

Edward Marsh, on his oath, saith :—

I was a sailor on the Wolverine in October, 1865, and went down with her to take troops to Morant Bay. On Friday, the 13th October (I think), we landed troops at Morant Bay and stayed there all night. On the following day we returned to Kingston, and went back again with arms. On that day, the 14th, we went from Morant Bay to Fort Morant in the Wolverine. Governor Eyre was then on board, I think. I think he came on board at Morant Bay on Saturday morning, 14th October. We embarked prisoners at night at Port Morant. From Port Morant we went to Port Antonio on Sunday the 15th October. Governor Eyre landed at

Port Antonio. We remained at Port Antonio the following day, Monday. They hanged one man before dinner on that day, and several after. I saw the first man hanged, and I saw several hanging afterwards. On one day I saw thirteen hanging. I can't say the day. We left Port Antonio on the Monday, and went to Port Morant. We returned to Port Antonio, I think, on the Wednesday. We then counted thirteen persons hanging on one pole. I don't know if Governor Eyre was at Port Antonio when we got back. I saw Mr. Gordon when he was brought on board. He was a prisoner. He was taken to Morant Bay in the Wolverine. He was some days on board. I took him ashore in the boat to Morant Bay. I can't say if Governor Eyre was then on board. I handed Mr. Gordon over to the Provost-marshal, Mr. Ramsay. I remember Dr. Bruce; he was a very old man. He was taken on board at Kingston. I landed him at Morant Bay. They didn't trouble about him, he was so old.

Cross-examined :—

I was only occasionally on shore when off duty. On the Sunday we towed a steamer back which we had seized, with 100 kegs. of gunpowder on board, and arms.

By the Court :—

Mr. Eyre landed on the Sunday at Port Antonio, and came on board again.

By defendant's Counsel :—

We took a General, La Motte, on board the steamer, and some Haytians, and put them on board the guard-ship Aboukir. I saw an American barque full of white refugees.

By the Court :—

We took the schooner the Sunday after we arrived; she had arms and ammunition, and a crew of nine or ten, besides the General.

Walter Rea, on his oath, saith :—

I was in Jamaica in October, 1865, seaman on board the Wolverine; we went to Morant Bay on the 12th October. The day after that the Governor came to Morant Bay. He came into the tent at night and read martial law to us from a paper. About 100 seamen and marines were in the tent. After reading martial law, the Governor said he hoped we should do our duty. The next morning I went with a party of seamen and marines to Easington, which is twenty-eight miles, I should think, from Morant Bay; there were thirty seamen and twenty marines. Lieutenant Oxley commanded us. We had our rifles and cutlasses and forty rounds of ammunition, and our orders were to shoot at any one we saw running away that we could not capture. These orders were obeyed in three cases on the way to Easington; the first was, we saw a man running behind some bushes on the coast, I should say twelve men fired at him, and wounded him; he ran into the sea, and Lieutenant O'Connor, of the marines, ran to the beach with his revolver and shot him. That man was not armed. I think he offered no resistance, he only tried to escape. The next case was a man playing a flute outside a cottage; he tried to run into the bush, and one man shot at and wounded him, another one afterwards shot him dead, and two of them then threw him up into the bush. This man offered no resistance, only when he saw us he ran away. I didn't hear him call out or say anything. After that the advanced-guard caught a man and passed him aft to the body of seamen; he tried to escape into the sugar-cane, and one marine shot him in the thigh and brought him down, and afterwards a sergeant shot him. He made no resistance and had no arms, he only said when the sergeant pointed at him, "Don't shoot, massa." We had about fifty prisoners in the rear, and some of them said this man had been seen in a market-place with a sugar-cane knife, the length of a cutlass, brandishing it about and trying to get the people to rebel. We got to Easington about four that afternoon; we took about fifty prisoners on the road. We met with no resistance at all on the road. At Easington we found no disturbance at all. We loopholed every window and shutter in the Court-house, and stationed men at each window and door. The police brought in prisoners at Easington and I twice mounted guard. Lieutenant Errington and Mr. Ramsay came there whilst I was at Easington. I was told to full-cock my rifle and fix my cutlass by Lieutenant Errington, and told if one man, who was condemned to die, should move or make the least resistance, I was to shoot him. He was afterwards shot by two men. There were three other men in the same room; one man had forty-eight lashes, and the other two were let off. We flogged a man who worked for Mr. Brown, and gave him three dozen because he would not bring the provisions up. We stayed at Easington four or five days, and brought a good many prisoners back to Morant Bay. They were all put in a tent and a black sentry put over them. After that our party was sent to Stoney Gut, about eleven miles from Morant Bay. I can't remember the day. We were sent off to Stoney Gut immediately. We went into the village; a female fired a pistol off and hit nobody, she was afterwards captured; there was no other resistance, there was nobody there; it was daybreak when we got there. We pulled down about twenty houses there that day. The next day a party of the 6th Foot were burning the houses, so we burnt houses. We cut down the bread-fruit and cocoa-nut trees. I think we remained three days at Stoney Gut; when we left all the houses were destroyed. I should say fifty or sixty houses altogether were destroyed. All the fruit-trees were cut down. We lived on the live stock, pigs and other animals, where we could catch them; some ran into the bush. After being three days at Stoney Gut we returned to Morant Bay; we went to Easington again for a day or two, and came back to Morant Bay. I saw twelve (I think) executions the day before we came off to the ship. I saw them hanged; they allowed us a quarter of an hour to see the men hanged. The men stood on a plank, and the piece that went across was a bamboo, and a man stood atop to make the rope fast. I saw Gordon in custody, but did not see him hanged.

Cross-examined :—

If a person got into the bush, you would never catch them, or in the sugar-cane. Our whole number, when we got to Stoney Gut, was 100 about. We had been increased. There were about 100 black soldiers, a battery of artillery, and the blue jackets and marines at Morant Bay. Stoney Gut would be a formidable position for an enemy to hold. It commanded the road to Kingston, and the bush surrounded it. It was not a plain country through which we marched, there was so much bush and wood. It was very rainy at this time, and the rivers much swollen, and that makes keeping communication open much more difficult. We had one or two of our horses and carts washed away, going to Easington. Stoney Gut is a somewhat inaccessible place to reach; we couldn't get artillery there. I should think we had great difficulty in getting a bag of biscuit there. We had to march there in single file. I don't think when we got there that Paul Bogle had been taken. We found females' dresses, and glass and china, they told us had come from Morant Bay. I should think the dresses were above the condition of the persons who lived at Stoney Gut. There is a place called White Horses, on the road to Easington; there was no marks of a disturbance there that I saw. I don't remember if there's a house there. It's a cliff, with a narrow road, and a deep valley. A sugar-knife is about three feet long, and very heavy; there were several found at Stoney Gut. Jamaica is very mountainous; they rise steeply from the shore; in some places there's a level country inland, and then the mountains begin again. The roads are generally in the track of the rivers; we had to cross about twelve going to Easington. In the summer the rivers are dry, and in the rainy season flooded. Hayti is about one day's sail from Jamaica.

By the Court :—

I have sailed to Hayti myself. None of the prisoners we took going to Easington had arms. We saw no one with arms going to Stoney Gut. It was dark. From the time that I landed at Morant Bay till I quitted that part of the country, I saw no disturbance.

Frederick Augustus Burt, being on his oath, saith :—

I was at Kingston, Jamaica, in October, 1855. I remember the time of the proclamation of martial law. There was then no outbreak or breach of the peace; nothing more than a little excitement from what had taken place at Morant Bay. The Courts of Justice were open, and so continued during the time martial law was proclaimed. On the 21st

October 1 was arrested by an ordinary policeman; he produced no warrant. He took me to the barracks on no charge whatever. I think two policemen joined him afterwards. I was locked up at the barracks. I requested to know what I was locked up for, and to see the custos and the superintendent of police. I saw neither, nor informed why, nor was I informed of any charge. When first taken to the barracks, I was put into an ordinary cell, and then removed by one of the officers to the guard-room, and had a mattress given me for the night. On Sunday 22nd, I was removed from the barracks, and taken to the Up Park Camp by a detachment of soldiers. At the camp I was put in a cell with two others; Signor Beneyiyne was one. I was there made to take off my boots; I received them again after a day or two. I know Dr. Bruce; he was brought into the same cell two or three days later. There was no bed or furniture in the cell. I was kept there a few days, and afterwards removed to   I saw men flogged, and I was ordered to witness it. Whilst in the cell, I was visited by Mr. Bicknell, the police magistrate of Kingston; he asked me a number of questions, and took down the answers. I requested to know what I was arrested for, and how long I should be detained. He told me he saw no reason for detaining me, and had he the power he'd release me at once. I was not so released. I afterwards saw General O'Connor. We were ordered out of our cells on the occasion of his visiting the camp. I asked him on what grounds I had been arrested, and told him that as an Englishman I thought I had a right to know. He did not appear to give any definite answer, but said he didn't know the grounds, and said I should not go back to the cells, but be taken to the officers' quarters. I was detained altogether twenty days. No charge was ever made against me. I had nothing in the least to do with the disturbance at Morant Bay. I know the handwriting of George William Gordon. The document shown to me is in his handwriting.

Cross-examined:—

I was about nine years in Jamaica. I think the population was 450,000. The country is thinly populated and scattered. I think there are nearly 400,000 black and coloured persons, and the rest white. I should think there were more than 13,000 whites, as stated in the census. I won't swear the census wasn't right.

Re-examined by the Court:—

The black population includes the Maroons. I think it was three or four days after my arrest that I saw Mr. Bicknell, and two days after that that I saw General O'Connor.

Alexander Phillips, on his oath, saith:—

I am a native of Jamaica, and lived there in 1865, in the Parish of

Vere and County of Middlesex. My residence was about forty-three miles from the nearest point of the district where martial law was proclaimed. I was not engaged in any business at the time. I had some freehold property. Directly or indirectly I had nothing whatever to do with the outbreak. I was arrested 24th October, 1865, by Lieutenant Sinclair, and a body of men, volunteers. No charge whatever was made against me. Lieutenant Sinclair informed me he was authorised by his Excellency the Governor to arrest me, search my house, and seize all my papers. I was put on horseback and conveyed to the Court-house at Alley, and placed in the custody of the military. I know Dr. Bruce, and had known him a long time. He lived in Vere, and I saw him in custody at Alley. He was under guard in a room apart from me. The next day he was put into a gig; he was handcuffed, and his left arm lashed to the gig with a rope. I was handcuffed, lashed with a rope, and put into a cart, and taken to Spanish Town. We stopped at Old Harbour, and had refreshment. It's thirty miles from Alley to Spanish Town. From Old Harbour Dr. Bruce was put into the same van as me. At Spanish Town is what is called the King's House, where Mr. Eyre lived. I was taken in front of that house. Lieutenant Sinclair was there, and he asked for his Excellency the Governor, and said he had brought the prisoners, Dr. Bruce, Phillips, and another. His Excellency said he was sorry we had met with such bad weather, and he ordered him to convey us to the Volunteer Station at Spanish Town, where we were accordingly taken. We remained there about three hours. Dr. Bruce's handcuffs were taken off; my rope was taken off, but I wore the handcuffs still, and so did the other prisoner, Morris. We were put into a carriage and conveyed to Up Park Camp, which was in the proclaimed district. We remained there that night and the following day, and about six in the evening we were taken to Kingston, put into a boat, and rowed to Port Royal, and put on board the Wolverine, and next morning we were taken to Morant Bay. Dr. Bruce was then delivered into the custody of Mr. Ramsay, who acted for the military as Provost-marshal. I saw Dr. Bruce again on 20th November; he was then in custody. He was released about the ast week in December. I was not in court when his case came on. After 20th December I saw him at Vere. I was sent to the cell in the prison amongst the prisoners who were called rebels. My handcuffs were taken off, but both hands were tied with rope, and I was kept in that state all the time. No charge whatever was ever made against me. I never inquired why I was detained, and I was never told; I never had the opportunity to inquire. I saw Gordon Ramsay during the time I was confined. I was released on 4th November; I was flogged and released. Four sailors were ordered to flog me; the orders were given by Lieutenant Adcock. I had a hundred lashes from a navy cat. I was not told at all why I was flogged. I did not ask why. I was only told to take off my lothes and receive a hundred lashes. I said to Lieutenant Adcock before the flogging commenced that it was impossible I could receive the flogging in my state of health. He requested to see my back. I showed it him, and he said I had a good back to receive it. I was in bad health at this time, and my health suffered most severely from the flogging. Lieutenant Adcock requested me to kneel after the flogging before him, and I did so. He requested me to bless the Queen and damn every black man. I did that. He told me to go and receive a pass, and go away. No doctor was present when I was flogged, and after it was over I went on the public road, and had to shift for myself. I had severe fever, and sat on the road side, unable to move, and a boy assisted me to put on my clothes. I went to far end of the bay, and sat under a bamboo tree in a fainting state with fever. My brother found me there, and he got me to a house, and it was some time before I was well enough to be removed to his house. I was confined in bed in this house two weeks with the severe wounds in my back, and then I returned home. I was never tried, nor told what I was arrested for. I didn't see persons flogged, but I heard a great number before I was flogged. I was afterwards tried by a special commission in February, 1866. The result was an acquittal. I was tried for conspiracy. Dr. Bruce was tried with myself and other prisoners. I was first subpœnaed in behalf of the Crown, and whilst waiting I was told I was indicted, and a true bill found against me. Dr. Bruce was acquitted also. Morris was not tried; he was flogged at Morant Bay. I saw some executions at Morant Bay; I was taken out, with other prisoners, to see them four times; I saw forty-nine executions; I saw Samuel Clark executed. Ten more were indicted with me for conspiracy; all were acquitted. The case was broken down for six of the prisoners. Four were sent for trial, Dr. Bruce, Levine, Kelly, Smith, and myself. The Attorney-General made a speech, and told the jury the men were indicted for conspiracy, but hoped they wouldn't link their names with Paul Bogle. The indictment charged us with conspiracy, with Bogle and others, to set aside the Queen's authority. Witnesses were called against me. Mr. Phillips was my counsel, and he spoke to the jury, who acquitted me.

Question put—Objected to by prosecuting Counsel:—

I have brought an action against Mr. Eyre. There is a fund formed to enable me to bring the action. I have not received any direct authority from Mr. Mill and Mr. Taylor to mention their names in getting subscriptions. I have seen the document now shown me before. I know Mr. Biggs and Mr. Camerovzow. They are not appointed by me or by my authority to collect subscriptions. Messrs. Shaen and Roscoe are my attorneys. Mr. Shaen never told me that permission had been obtained for me to use Messrs. Taylor and Mill's names in recommending me for subscriptions. Mr. Camerovzow told me so, and that he was treasurer to the fund and also Mr. Pringle, my agent, told me so. I think it was in March last that I knew of this fund being commenced. I have been ten months in this country. I have received some assistance from the fund that is raised for me, not from any other source. I draw on Mr. Shaen for what money I require. I began to draw upon him last year, I think in August. Mr. Shaen paid my expenses from Jamaica here. I was examined twice before the Royal Commissioners. I mentioned Ensign Taylor, but I never mentioned Lieutenant Adcock before the Commissioners, because I did not know his name.

Re-examined :—

I have nothing whatever to do with this present prosecution. I have been subpœnaed, and I am come in consequence of that. I did not volunteer to come at all. I was subpœnaed three different times. I have had nothing to do with the criminal proceedings; it's only my action I am concerned. I used Ensign Taylor's name as the person of whom I received the pass, his being the only name I knew of the officers. I produce the pass.

Edward Fairfield, on his oath, saith :—

I am a clerk in the Colonial Office, and produce certain despatches—page 98 in the blue book—Disturbances, Pt. 1. I produce the despatch and enclosure. Enclosure numbered 4 read. Bruce, Morris, and Phillips are referred to in the margin. Enclosure No. 5 also read. Enclosure No. 1, read by Mr. Giffard, is correct. Enclosure No. 7, page 100, read by Mr. Giffard, is correct. Enclosure No. 9, also read by Mr. Giffard. Enclosure No. 12, read by Mr. Giffard, is right. Enclosure numbered 16, read by Mr. Giffard. Enclosure No. 20 (telegraphic), read by Mr. Giffard; it is not dated. Enclosure No. 21, also read. Enclosure No. 23, read. Enclosure No. 24, read. Enclosure No. 27, read. Enclosure No. 28, read. Enclosure No. 29, read. Enclosure 1, read by Sir Robert Collier, and answered to the same despatch, 275, page 149 in the blue book. Enclosure No. 6, read. Enclosure 7, No. 25, read; fifteen persons are there entered, "released, being deemed innocent." Enclosure No. 8, read by Sir R. Collier. Enclosure No. 9, read by Sir R. Collier. Enclosure No. 10, dated October 21st, also read. Page 157, enclosure 18, read by Sir R. Collier. Enclosure 20, also read. Enclosure 21, also read. Enclosure 4, read by Mr. Giffard. Enclosure 11, read by Mr. Giffard. Enclosure 13, read by Mr. Giffard. Enclosure 14, read by Mr. Giffard. Enclosure 15, part read, which is a list of prisoners. Enclosure No. 16, read by Mr. Giffard. I cannot find despatch No. 210; it is mislaid. The bill produced was found in the bundle of depositions on the trial of Mr. Gordon. That bill is now read.

Charles Savil Roundell, sworn :—

I have handed all the documents I had to the Colonial Office. Mr. Fairfield here produces a letter, dated 22nd October, 1865, which I know to be in Mr. Eyre's handwriting. It is now read. I was present when

Mr. Eyre was examined. I had something to do with making up part of the blue book. I had to do with the appendix, not the part now shown to me. I had the printed transcript of Mr. Eyre's evidence. Mr. Eyre was examined from printed papers, and I had them in my possession ; amongst them the printed paper headed, "The State of the Island." have no doubt the copies I had were destroyed.

James Drover Barnett, sworn, and being cross-examined, saith:—

I took notes of evidence given by Mr. Eyre, on the forty-seventh day, Tuesday, 20th March, 1866. I think he was examined that entire day, and part of the next.

William Shaen, sworn, being cross-examined, saith:—

I have seen the original of the letter now put into my hand.* I sent it for insertion, by direction of Mr. Mill, given me on the previous day. Dr. Bruce commenced an action against Mr. Eyre. The writ was first in the Court of Exchequer ; no further proceedings were taken, and it expired. A month or two afterwards another was issued in the Queen's Bench ; that has been discontinued a month or two back. Dr. Bruce is now in Jamaica. I have not been paid his cost. I have a fund applicable to the funds given me by friends of his. Mr. Mill and Mr. Taylor have never contributed a penny to that fund. I have seen a circular in which they recommended Mr. Phillips for subscriptions. There are some subscribers to the fund I could mention, and some I would rather not. The Jamaica Committee, as a body, have declined to have anything to do with the action. It had never been explained to them that they would be liable for Mr. Eyre's costs.

Re-examined:—

I have not received any instructions relating to the actions from Messrs. Mill and H. Taylor, and I have not professionally communicated with them about the actions. Mr. Phillips was unwilling to come as a witness, and I subpœnaed him.

John Gorrie, sworn, and being cross-examined, saith:—

The Act of Indemnity (Jamaica) was allowed by order in Privy Council. All laws of Jamaica require confirmation by the Privy Council. Until disallowed by Privy Council, all Acts are law. The Act authorising detention, &c. (29 Vict. chap. 2), was passed. I can't say the date. It was disallowed 16th January, 1866, and was law up to that time. The venue of an indictment in Morant Bay would be St. Thomas-in-the-East, and that is not in the district of Kingston. The Provost-marshal in Jamaica is what is here called a Sheriff.

---

* A Letter of Mr. Buxton's, published in the papers.

Re-examined :—

I have a note of the Acts authorising the Governor to issue Special Commissions. There is one Act 23 Vic. chap. 15. I now read the first section of that Act. There were former statutes to the same effect and one later:—5 Wm. 4, cap. 18, sec. 2 ; 4 Geo. 4, cap. 13, sec. 6 ; 33 Charles 2, cap. 8 ; 23 Vic., cap. 3 ; and 29 Vic., cap. 6, are statutes referring to Special Commissions.

This deponent, Edward Fairfield, on his oath, further saith as follows :—

I now produce a despatch, dated 22nd August, and appearing in page 256 of Papers relating to Papers in Jamaica. The postscript to that despatch is now read by Sir R. Collier. I produce also the proceedings in manuscript, and partly printed, in the court-martial upon Mrs. Gordon. They are put in.

In addition to the above oral evidence, various documents and extracts from the examination of Mr. Eyre before the Royal Commissioners were put in, and were marked by the magistrate in the Blue Book as in evidence.

I. Parliamentary Papers on Disturbances in Jamaica, Part I., p. 98 and p. 100 ; Despatch 275, p. 149 ; and Enclosures and Despatch 256, 22nd August.

II. Examination of Mr. Eyre, printed in the Minutes of Evidence before the Royal Commission 31st January, 1866, and 20th March, 1866, p. 981 ; with the various communications referred to by Mr. Eyre as received by him.* Of these documents, far too voluminous to be inserted *in extenso*, the substance is as follows :—

In the examination of Mr. Eyre he first gave a great deal of evidence as to the condition of the colony *prior* to the outbreak, and as to the *previous* apprehensions of a rebellion. He stated :—

In April, 1865, I wrote to the Secretary of State transmitting the statement of distress and grievances from certain poor people of St. Anne's, and then wrote thus :—" This is the first fruits of Dr. Underhill's letter, which represented the peasantry of Jamaica as being generally in a destitute, naked, and starving condition—a representation which many of them

---

* The magistrates only admitted portions, but the learned Judge, it will be seen, told the Grand Jury emphatically to read *the whole*.

will be quite ready to take advantage of, and to turn to their own account in every way they can ; nor will there be wanting persons in this colony to encourage and urge them on ; and I fear that the result of Dr. Underhill's communication and the circulars of the Baptist Missionary Society will have a very prejudicial influence in unsettling the minds of the peasantry, making them discontented with their lot, and disinclined to conform to the laws, which they have been told are unjust." (Evidence of Mr. Eyre, page 83.) That, he said, was his conviction as far back as April, 1865 ; and that was the first letter he wrote showing his conviction that a system of agitation had been introduced which would have a very injurious effect on the future of the colony. (Ibid.) There were, he added, many other subsequent despatches to the like effect, and one of them, dated the 22nd of August, 1865, was also put in evidence and contained these passages (Parliamentary Papers on Jamaica, p. 256) :—

" It is clear that if the ministers of religion residing among an ignorant, debased, and excitable coloured population take upon themselves to endorse and reiterate assertions such as those in Dr. Underhill's letter, to the effect that the people are starving, ragged, and naked ; that all this arises from taxation being too heavy, and that such taxation is unjust upon the coloured population ; that they are refused just tribunals and denied political rights—then such ministers do their best not only to make the labourer discontented, but to stimulate sedition and resistance to the constituted authorities and the law. Nor should I be surprised if, in the districts where such a course is taken, a refusal to pay the taxes and consequent disturbances in enforcing them should be the result. I have just had put into my hands by the Baron von Kettelhodt an inflammatory address, which has been printed and circulated among the people of St. Thomas-in-the-East (of which the Baron is custos) prior to a meeting which has lately taken place there. This document shows the manner in which a few evil-disposed agitators get up public meetings in support of Dr. Underhill, and the spirit in which the promoters prepared the populace beforehand. The Baron informs me that he has good reason to believe that George William Gordon either wrote or was concerned in getting up the printed address now forwarded." (Parl. Papers, 256.)

There was enclosed the proclamation or placard issued by Gordon, which is also set out at length in the "Evidence of Mr. Eyre" (p. 88), headed " State of the Island : "—
"People of St. Thomas-in-the-East,—You have been ground down too long. Shake off your sloth, and we advise you to be up and doing," &c.
This was originally issued and dated on the 29th of July, 1865 ; the evidence admitted as to this matter was as follows :—Mr. Eyre stated in the examination that " this was the paper in which the persons were named who were the victims of the massacre in October," and that he " had ascertained, through the postmistress, that it had been circulated by

Gordon" (Minutes of Evidence, page 90), and the proceedings on the trial of Gordon were put in evidence, and there it appeared that it was deposed by the postmistress as follows :—"For some time past Mr. Gordon has been carrying on a regular correspondence with Chisholm M'Laren. He wrote M'Laren, I think, about two posts before the breaking out on Wednesday at Morant Bay. I have also seen letters pass through the post-office from him to Bogle, but not very often. The last one to M'Laren was very thick, not a single letter. I have received a packet of printed papers addressed in Mr. Gordon's handwriting to Paul Bogle, and another to Chisholm. They came by the post shortly after the publication of the Queen's address. I read one of the printed papers out of the packet addressed to Bogle. I had one at the post-office at Morant Bay at the time of the outbreak ; the heading of it was 'To the People of St. Thomas-in-the-East and St. Anne's.' It called upon the people to be 'up and doing." (Minutes of Evidence, p. 620.) Such was the evidence on this point at the trial of Gordon. It has been stated that the address was originally dated and issued on almost the last day in July, and there was a great deal of evidence put in to show that apprehensions had been largely entertained of a negro rising intended for the 1st of August, but that it had been prevented by the prompt measures taken, and that then it was put off till October. The evidence on this head admitted by the magistrate consisted of official statements made by Mr. Eyre as to the information he had and the measures he had taken, and also of communications he had actually received from various parts of the island, stating the apprehensions which were entertained. The official documents admitted in evidence were these :—On the 24th of July the Governor wrote to the Secretary of State, transmitting a communication from the Custos of St. Elizabeth, enclosing documents representing that there was an apprehension that riot or rebellion would break out in some of the parishes at the commencement of August (the anniversary of freedom), on the ground of unjust taxation, and stating that, "should this be so, it will be due entirely to Dr. Underhill's letter, and to the delusions which have been instilled into the minds of the ignorant peasantry by designing persons in reference to it."

" Every effort" (wrote Mr. Eyre) "will be made to prepare for and guard against the contingency suggested; nor do I myself anticipate any serious outbreak." The Custos of St. Elizabeth, however, on the 28th of July, wrote to the Governor in these terms :—

"From all I can gather there is no doubt that an insurrection to rob and burn was decided on, and that strong and severe measures will be necessary. The general opinion among proprietors—white, coloured, and black—is that all the disturbance and ill-feeling is to be attributed to the late assertions that the negroes are cheated and ill-treated, and that if permitted to be reiterated there will be no security for life or property."

Measures were accordingly taken, a ship-of-war was sent round ; the 1st of August passed over without a rising. On that day the Custos of St. Elizabeth wrote to the Governor, thanking him for the measures adopted for putting down the evil feeling which, he firmly believed, prevailed throughout the country, adding that so widespread a belief and so common a subject of public talk must have had rise in some intention to do evil. Policemen and rural constables have been threatened as to what would be their fate in the August week. (Minutes of Evidence, 984.)

And on the 4th of August the Custos again wrote to the like effect, reporting that no disturbance had yet occurred, and that he had received many reports, but, as yet, no evidence sufficient to enable him to go beyond suspicion.

"The intention to do some wrong is" (he wrote) "clear, and generally understood through this part of the country, and steps taken to meet and put down any disturbance had maintained quiet, and prevented an outbreak. The presence of her Majesty's ship 'Bull Dog' has had an excellent effect. There is no disturbance, but a feeling of insecurity, and a fear of fire which is said to have been threatened." (Minutes of Evidence, 985). On the other hand the Custos of Westmoreland wrote that "order continued to prevail through that parish, and he saw no cause to apprehend any disturbance." (Ibid.)

"But considerable alarm seems to prevail among the gentlemen residing near the parish from the serious reports which reach them from the adjacent parish of St. Elizabeth. This has been shown by the application made to the merchants of Savanna-la-Mer for gunpowder for the purpose of self-defence." (Ibid.)

Other letters put in from other parts of the country ascribed the alarm to rumours—which, however, had so far a foundation that they were actually got up by evil-disposed persons who were ready to take advantage of them. Thus a magistrate from Montego Bay stated the rumours of expected disturbances, but added that he could not say that he had seen or heard anything showing any combination among the labouring classes for any acts of violence. (Evidence, p. 984.)

"It seems to me that there is a feeling among the labouring population, which has been probably created by exaggeration or actual misrepresentation, by some mischievous persons, of remarks made at recent meetings and arising out of them, that they are being severely oppressed by the high prices of goods and provisions, and the low rates of wages, and by taxation." "I fear," the writer added, "that there are a few evil-disposed persons who seize the opportunity to try and create a bad feeling, or dissatisfaction, or to extend any that may exist ; and they assist in getting up or in circulating some of the rumours that are about. There are some who maliciously point their remarks against individuals, for certain individuals are, somehow, constantly named as being marked out for attack. Until these rumours began to circulate, there seemed no reason whatever to suspect that the labouring population was otherwise than peaceably disposed." (Ibid.) On the 5th of August the same gentleman wrote to the like effect :—"It is still rumoured that there is to be resistance in some shape to the payment of taxes, but as yet it is but rumour. No doubt the high prices of all classes of provisions have been of late severely felt. I have never known every description of food to be at such high prices all at the same time. At such a time, as is well known, the poorer classes are far more easily excited to feelings of discontent, and at such a time much mischief may be done by a few evil-disposed mischievous persons." (Ibid.) Then an article in the *County Union* of the 12th of September, 1865, was put in, the effect of which was to suggest that if the taxation was kept up the people would be goaded to desperation. (Minutes of Evidence, p. 986.) And Mr. Eyre, in his examination, put in a letter from the editor of the same paper (one Levine, who was one of those ordered by him to be arrested), stating that he was acting editorially for the purpose of screening Dr. Bruce (another of those he arrested) "and others from the charge of anarchy and tumult which must necessarily follow from the very strong demonstrations which have been made," alluding to meetings which had been held. (Minutes of Evidence, p. 89.) Mr. Eyre, in his statement, proceeded to say that the first apprehension brought under his notice of disturbances likely to occur was prior to August, 1865, and he took immediate measures by sending a man-of-war round, and directing the local authorities to take such other steps as they could on the spot; and the taking of these measures, he thought, prevented the disturbances at that time. No disturbances broke out, at all events, until the outbreak of October, 1865.

Such was the evidence as to the state of the colony up to the time of the outbreak.

It appeared from the evidence that the first intimation Mr. Eyre received of the impending outbreak was from the unfortunate Baron Ketelholdt, one of the victims of the massacre, who on the 10th, the day before the massacre, wrote to the Governor a private letter, stating the riot and rescue which had that day occurred :—

"I am sorry to say that Mr. G. W. Gordon's inflammatory addresses have borne fruit earlier than I had anticipated. On my arrival here I found the respectable people in a great state of alarm and excitement, in consequence of demonstrations of disaffection and open violence by a body of men who came down to the Court-house armed with bludgeons. . The ringleader in this affair is a man of the name of Bogle, who generally acts with Mr. G. W. Gordon." (Minutes of Evidence, page 1,003-4.)

On the 11th of October, 1865, Mr. Eyre received intelligence of the massacre at Morant Bay, in which 28 persons were murdered and the Courthouse burnt, and further that the insurgents were going on. (Minutes of

Evidence, p. 84.) The outbreak occurred at 3 o'clock on the afternoon of the 11th of October, and Mr. Eyre stated that on the 12th of October several communications reached him notifying that the negroes had fulfilled their expressed intention of going down to the Bay on the 11th; that they had risen in insurrection and had killed the Custos, several of the magistrates, the inspector of police, the commanding officer of the volunteers, and others, had released the prisoners from gaol, and had burnt down the Court-house. It was further (he said) reported that the insurgents intended to proceed with their work of devastation up the line of Blue Mountain Valley. On the evening of the same day Mr. Eyre stated he had an interview with a magistrate who lived some eight miles from Morant Bay, and who had just made his escape from the district in insurrection, and reported that the same morning a party of negroes, armed with cutlasses and sticks, had entered his house and threatened to kill him and another gentleman who was at the house, and all white or coloured persons, and that while escaping he saw about 1000 people armed with cutlasses and sticks, with flags flying, drums beating, and horns blowing, all going toward Morant Bay; and subsequently saw other parties similarly armed. These facts, Mr. Eyre stated, were reported to him on the evening of the 12th, and with these facts before him, and remembering also that about two months before he had been compelled to send ships-of-war and take other steps to prevent anticipated risings in another part of the island, and aware that disaffection and agitation had sedulously been stirred up throughout the entire colony, and knowing well the character of the black population, and their proneness to act upon impulse and follow examples, he could have no doubt (he said) "that a very serious rebellion had broken out, and that it was his duty to proclaim martial law, as the only means of meeting so grave an emergency." (Answer of Mr. Eyre to Question 46,578, Minutes of Evidence before the Royal Commissioners, p. 990.) Early on the 13th of October the Council of War assembled, and under the statutory law of the colony agreed to proclaim martial law, there being present, with the Governor, the Commander-in-chief, the Chief Justice, the Attorney-General, and the leading magistrates and members of the House of Assembly, all of whom were unanimous for martial law. On the 13th, with the assent and advice of the Council, the Governor declared martial law under a local Act which authorised it. The proclamation declared—

"That martial law should prevail throughout the county of Surrey, except Kingston, and that the military forces should have the power of exercising the rights of belligerents against such of the inhabitants as the military might consider opposed to the Government." (Evidence, p. 83.)

Mr. Eyre further stated that on the 13th of October, the day martial law was proclaimed, he received a letter from a magistrate at Port Antonio (the opposite end or corner of the same side of the island as Morant Bay), stating the apprehensions there entertained that the insurgents would probably be there that night, and begging for aid, urging that "every hour was of the utmost importance." The acts of Mr. Eyre in the meanwhile appeared on his own statement as follows :—On the 12th the Governor went to Morant Bay, and on the 14th several prisoners were tried by court-martial while he was there, though he was not, so far as appeared, actually present either at the trials or the executions. The Attorney-General sat on the first court-martial held. Information was received that the rebels were going to burn Port Antonio, and the Governor went there. (Evidence, p. 86.) While he was there on the 16th, twenty-seven prisoners were tried by court-martial and executed. (Evidence, p. 86.) Parties of military had meanwhile been sent out in different directions, under officers.

As to acts done by the military here it may be mentioned that it was proved by several of the witnesses for the prosecution that prisoners were taken who were not actually "found in arms," and that they were shot ; but it did not appear that Mr. Eyre had even known of these acts until afterwards. He stated in his examination as follows :—

That the reports he received were comparatively brief, that the officers never reported to him, but to the Commander-in-chief, and that, therefore, when he was in the neighbourhood, these reports were shown to him, yet that, as to a considerable number of them, he only received copies just in time to send to the Secretary of State, and that as to many he had never seen them. (Evidence, p. 87.) He directed, he said, the movements of the troops while he was with them, but with the subsequent details he had nothing to do—that was left entirely to the military powers. He gave no directions whatever (beyond what has been stated), understanding that during martial law the supreme power was vested in the military authorities. (Evidence, p. 87.) It appeared, however, that on the 18th of October Mr. Eyre gave a memorandum of direction to General Nelson, which was in these terms :—

"In the present state of the insurrection, and of the plans for putting it down, it appears, then, that the district in which the rebels are most in force lies between the military post of Manchioneal and the station recently evacuated at Easington. I am of opinion that the most effectual position to occupy for present purposes would be Fort Antonio at Manchioneal, Morant Bay, and Easington. I think that 150 Maroons should be armed and placed under Colonel Fyfe, and sent, in two divisions—one to act in the dreetion of Morant Bay, or towards Blue Mountain Valley ; the other towards Bath Plantain Garden and Manchioneal, each scouring the hills, and the outskirts of the cultivated lands, to drive in, cut off, or capture the rebels ;

if they have retired from the lowlands or lands contiguous. If they thus act in co-operation with the military authorities at Port Antonio, Manchioneal, Morant Bay, and Kingston, I think the country will be completely secured, and those in arms against the Queen be either cut off or captured—a step which is essential prior to the declaration of an amnesty. . . . . . I think arms and ammunition should be left at Morant Bay to be distributed among a party of planters and others who are prepared to arm from Kingston and re-establish themselves on the Plantain Garden River or Bath districts, if armed. . . . There is a settlement (a few miles from Morantown) where several white and coloured families reside, and are apprehensive of danger ; this post should be visited. " (Evidence p. 87.)

These, Mr. Eyre stated, were the instructions he gave to General Nelson, and which were carried out, and this was put in by the prosecution as rendering him responsible for what these different parties of soldiers actually did in various districts. As to which, however, there was no evidence that he even knew of them, or of any other orders or directions than those above stated. At this point comes the oral evidence already given as to Mr. Eyre being at Morant Bay or other places at the time trials by court-martial and executions were going on ; but there was no evidence that he directed the trials or knew of the proceedings of the courts, or the charges or the evidence on which they proceeded. It appeared, however, in evidence that as to all the trials by court-martial they were entirely under military authority ; for a subsequent minute of the military commanders was put in, stating that they declined to try certain prisoners (Bruce and Levine) whom Mr. Eyre had ordered to be arrested and sent to Morant Bay with a view to their being tried by martial law for sedition, their reasons being—" that the prisoners all uttered the sentiments which were said to be seditious prior to the rebellion ;" and it did not appear that they had any immediate connection with it. (Parliamentary Papers on Disturbances, part 1, page 157.) The General in command of the district wrote to this effect to the Commander-in-Chief, and he approved, and refused to allow the men to be tried. So it appeared by the proceedings put in, that in Gordon's case, as in others, the trial was under military authority. It was proved that, in order to show it was unnecessary, that at the time mentioned there was no outbreak or disturbance—*i.e.*, at Morant Bay, where the witness was, and where the trial was held, and where the military were in actual occupation, but no evidence was given to show that the rest of the district was restored to peace. Nor did it appear that the trial was by Mr. Eyre's orders, or that he was in the place at the time. It was proved, as already stated, that the ordinary tribunals were sitting at Kingston, but not at Morant Bay, the place of the trial. It was not proved that Mr. Eyre directed the execution of the sentence, and by the proceedings it appeared that it was directed by the military commander. As to the other case of capital punishment, the case of Marshall, executed by order of the Provost-marshal, it did not appear that Mr. Eyre had known of it or had given the Provost-marshal any directions or authority. These cases occurred between the 17th and 24th October, and in that interval it appeared, from the oral evidence already given, Mr. Eyre had directed the arrest of several persons: Bruce, Levine, Phillips, Vinen, &c. But it appeared from the printed evidence that in September Levine, the editor of a paper, had written to Bruce:—

"I am writing articles to guard you from the charge of anarchy and tumult which must necessarily result from the very strong demonstrations which have been made." (Evidence, p. 89.)

In vindication of these arrests Mr. Eyre made certain statements as to the condition of the colony at the time, especially as to military force :—

At the time those arrests were made there were only 1,000 troops in the colony altogether, 500 of which were kept in the disturbed district, and could not be removed ; the other 500 were engaged in defending

Kingston and other places, and there were apprehensions (he said) of disturbances arising not only there, but elsewhere, and in almost every part of the island the whole island was considered in the most imminent danger. There was not a single soldier who could be detached to any one district, if any further outbreak had occurred (which was considered imminent), and on that conviction he considered himself justified in taking the most prompt and summary measures. (Evidence, p. 90.)

Mr. Eyre justified this conviction by producing before the Commissioners a vast number of communications he had received about this time from every part of the island, expressing the utmost alarm, and praying for the protection of the military:—

On the 19th of October, a letter from a leading magistrate and member of Assembly (Mr. Hosack) to the Governor, dated Kingston, October 19, stated that three persons had been taken into custody, and that he was of opinion that the Haytians should also have been taken into custody and deported, as "a great rebellion was going on in Hayti, and rebellion is a hydra-headed monster, on which heads often grow as fast as they are cut of." This letter stated that Kingston was quiet and well guarded, and that the promptness of the Governor and the troops was rapidly restoring confidence, but that Kingston was still the point to which families were flying from all parts. (Minutes of Evidence before the Commissioners, p. 992.) The utmost evidence that could be obtained, even from the most excited witnesses, was that ten or twelve persons had been drilled with wooden guns. The demonstration made by the volunteers, backed by the presence of a vessel of war, had (it is said) done much good; but, as already mentioned, the Custos adhered to his opinion as to the necessity for precautionary measures. (Vickers to Jordan, Minutes of Evidence, p. 995.)

This letter, dated the 23rd of October, was the last marked by the magistrate as to be deemed as evidence (though in the Minutes of Evidence there are a long series of similar letters up to the 12th of November), and, therefore, none others are here quoted, though the learned Judge told the Grand Jury to look at the *whole*.

Mr. Eyre, in his answer to Question 46,578, the whole of which was admitted as evidence, alluded to the *whole* period of the duration of martial law, and concluded thus:—"I proceed to state the particulars of the circumstances brought to the notice of the Government." (Minutes of Evidence, p. 991.) The next and last letter admitted by the magistrate is one from the Custos of Westmoreland to the Government Secretary, dated the 23rd of October, commencing—"Since writing to you on the 19th," and ending, "as regards the necessity for precautionary measures being adopted to guard against any serious riots at the Circuit Court, I am still of the opinion conveyed in my letter to you of the 19th," but which letter, as the magistrate has not marked it as in evidence, the reporter cannot quote. That of the 23rd, referring to it, and which is in evidence, and is the last letter admitted in evidence, states that on the 20th, after consulting with the magistrates at Savanna-la-Mer, it was determined, on account of the serious rumours from the Bluefields district, and the state of alarm in which the town was placed, to assemble the volunteers and thus "bring matters to a crisis" before the alleged rioters obtained strength. Many other communications were put in by Mr. Eyre before the Commissioners between the 19th and 23rd of October, but none of them were marked by the magistrate as to be deemed in evidence in this proceeding until the 23rd of October, when there was one to the Governor from a Mr. Williams, a magistrate, to the Governor, enclosing a communication from a gentleman living in St. Elizabeth, urgently asking for assistance, and stating, that "the people about me are in a very excited state; but I have no fear of their rising, so long as they are left to themselves. However, as G. W. Gordon often lives here and has a large Baptist chapel about three miles from my house, where he has lately been holding forth in his usual strain, I shall not feel at ease until all is quiet." (Minutes of Evidence, p. 994.) The letter to the Governor enclosing this stated :—

"The district is a stronghold of Mr. Gordon's, densely populated by a disorderly set of vagabonds; and he (the writer of the enclosed letter) may be in more danger than he thinks. I have written to him to say that, should there be an outbreak, his efforts for protection would be useless; and that if he feels himself in danger he should immediately bring his family down to Spanish Town. I would suggest that, as the district is the only one where strong excitement exists in relation to Mr. Gordon, whether 50 or 60 white troops should not immediately be located there before an insurrection should arise." (Minutes of Evidence, p. 994.)

This was on the 23rd of October (the day of Gordon's execution), and on the same day the Government Secretary had another letter from the same place in these terms:—

"The dreadful atrocities perpetrated in St. Thomas-in-the-East induces me to address you, requesting that you will bring to the Governor's notice the unprotected state of this district, in the event of any outbreak among the people, there not being any organised body in existence, the volunteers having resigned some time ago, &c. . . . . I may as well mention that Mr. G. W. Gordon visited this district about two months ago, and I am creditably informed that he, in addressing a meeting in a church, used such seditious language that the pastor had to stop him. He then left, and went to his property about three miles from the place, and there is no telling what amount of sedition he spread there." (Allen to Jordan, Minutes of Evidence, p. 995.)

On the 23rd of October it appeared that Mr. Eyre had to send an armed force to protect the circuit courts. At this date occurred the execution of Gordon, who had been arrested on the 17th, and was tried on the 21st of October and executed on the 23rd. The evidence adduced against Mr. Eyre on the matter, mainly consisted of the statements extracted from him in his examinations before the Royal Commissioners, which are as follows :—

Mr. Eyre stated that it was by his directions Gordon was apprehended; that he was not at the time within the proclaimed district, but that his ordinary residence was within it, and that there was first an attempt to arrest him at his ordinary residence, but it was found that he was hiding at Kingston, which was not proclaimed. Mr. Eyre further stated that at the time he gave directions for him to be apprehended, he had heard, in the disturbed district, from every quarter, and had reason to believe, from various little facts and circumstances (such as his issuing seditious placards under the plea of advising the people, and his being intimately connected with all the chief rebels, and various other little facts of that kind), that he had been the prime mover of the outbreak; and he found the same opinion was universally entertained in Kingston. Among other things, he was informed that some of the rebels had stated that he was the cause of their being brought to the gallows. He had reason, he said, to believe that it was his acts and his language which had led to the rebellion. "That is to say," interposed the Commissioners, "had excited it." (Examination of Mr. Eyre, Memorandum of Evidence, pp. 88, 89.) Pressed by them as to any information tending to show that he was "the instigator of this particular outbreak," Mr. Eyre answered that "he had circulated seditious placards, mentioning by name those individuals who were subsequently murdered, whom he held up to odium." (Ibid.) He particularly referred to the address headed 'The State of the Island,' originally issued on the 29th July, as already mentioned, but which Mr. Eyre stated he had since ascertained had been circulated by Gordon (Ibid.), and copies of which were found in the post-office just after the time of the outbreak.

(Evidence on Gordon's trial, Minutes of Evidence, vide Nelson's evidence.) Such was the evidence as to Mr. Eyre's act in directing the arrest of Gordon. The next evidence on this head was as to the trial, as to which the Minutes of Evidence were put in (Minutes of Evidence, p. 617), whence it appeared that the trial was on the 21st of October, at Morant Bay, on a charge that he had excited the insurgents, and by his conference with them tended to cause the rebellion, riot, or insurrection of the 11th of October; and it appeared that on the trial one.Anderson swore that he heard Gordon say at Stoney Gut to Bogle (the active leader in the massacre), "We must get up some men for to go to Morant Bay to seek about the backlands, and if we don't get the backlands all the buckra (*i.e.*, the whites) they will be die (*i.e.*, all be killed)." And the address of Gordon, headed "The State of the Island," seized at the post-office at Morant Bay, on the 11th of October, was put in, containing these words: "We advise you to be up and doing." &c., and particularly naming the principal persons massacred, Ketelholdt and others. And the post-mistress at Morant Bay, one of the witnesses, stated that Gordon had corresponded with Bogle, and that she had received a packet of printed papers addressed to Bogle in Gordon's handwriting shortly after the publication of the Queen's advice, and that she had read one of the printed papers addressed to Bogle, and she had it in the post-office at the time of the outbreak, and it was headed, "To the people of St. Thomas-in-the-East," and called upon the people to be "up and doing" (Minutes of Evidence, p. 640.) (As regards the evidence in the case, of which these appear to form the principal points, it is not necessary here to say more.) It appeared from the Minutes of the trial (put in evidence) that the court-martial assembled "by order of General Nelson," and that the General "approved and confirmed." Moreover, it also appeared that he reported the proceedings not to the Governor, but to the Commander-in-chief; and that the latter having sent the proceedings to the Governor, the latter returned them with these words:—"I have duly seen the proceedings of the Court, and fully concur in the justice of the sentence, and also the policy of carrying it into effect." (Minutes of Evidence, p. 91.) But it was stated also by Mr. Eyre, which was put in evidence, and also appeared from a letter of his, which likewise forms part of the evidence in the present proceedings, that before sentence was carried out, the proceedings were remitted to the Commander-in-chief of the colony, having been in fact first received by him, and approved by him before being sent to the Governor. (Minutes of Evidence, pp. 1,017-18.)

The execution of Gordon was on the 23rd. Bogle and the other active leaders of the insurrection were executed on the 24th of October, and it may be proper here to introduce certain communications put in evidence as received by Mr. Eyre, between the 23rd and the 30th, the date of the amnesty :—

"On the 23rd Mr. Eyre received a letter from Westmoreland parish as to anticipated disturbances at the approaching circuit court. "With the present jury system," said the writer, "whatever may be the evidence, it is anticipated that an acquittal will be the result, upon which it is not unlikely that a popular outbreak will be the result. To obviate this apprehended danger to the public peace, it is contemplated to change the *venue*. This would be for many reasons impolitic and unwise. Now that a rebellious spirit is openly exhibited it should not be smothered, but should be allowed to manifest itself wherever so disposed, especially as the Government are in arms and prepared to cope with it. To exhibit a temporising spirit would be fatal to the future peace of society; the manifestation of a determined will to suppress and punish this lawlessness will effect more good, and inspire a more wholesome fear and respect than the course which is counselled of seceding from the ordinary course of law in order to avow possible consequences of irritation to a disaffected mob. If, as is not unlikely, local and class prejudices may secure a verdict which reason and justice cannot sanction, that will afford but an illustration of the vices of the present judicial system, so as to call for the action of Government in its correction, but the threat—which, as I learn, has been openly hazarded—that the mob will do themselves justice if the law fails to give it, ought in these times not to be overlooked; and the Government should be prepared to teach a lesson that it is not by these means that redress of wrongs is to be accomplished." Upon which Mr. Eyre endorsed a minute that he quite concurred, and that the civil executive would be prepared to meet whatever emergency arose. (Minutes of Evidence, p. 996.) On the same day the senior magistrate of Hanover parish wrote a long letter, stating that "there is good reason for knowing that a spirit of disaffection exists among the lower orders, and there is no knowing how soon or how fatally it may be roused into action. (Ibid.) If such an event were to occur, it would find us perfectly unprepared and entirely helpless. There is not (irrespective of the police) a stand of arms in the place, and no ammunition (except the little in the stores of persons who deal in it), and there can be little doubt that at present the town, with lives and valuable property therein, would become an easy prey to a mob of far inferior strength to that so suddenly collected at Morant Bay." On the 25th of October, Lieutenant Irvine wrote from Port Antonio to inform the Governor that on the previous day a schooner was seized—having on board 100 kegs of gunpowder and five Haytian passengers (General La Motte and others)—for not giving a satisfactory explanation for being here when she cleared out from Kingston on the 9th. Fire arms were found on board, which were loaded. (Minutes of Evidence, p. 997.) On the same day a gentleman wrote from Montego Bay, conveying alarm as to an outbreak, and stating "The volunteers and special constables would scarcely be able to effect much against a thousand armed and infuriated savages. The chief part from among a people proverbial, from the large admixture of the African elements, for turbulence and ferocity." (Minutes of Evidence, p. 998.) And the Clerk of the Peace wrote: "In the event of the disturbance here, the authorities are (if I accept such aid as a handful of volunteers could give) absolutely powerless." (Ibid.) Next day the Governor wrote to the Commander-in-Chief to send troops to Savanna-la-Mer. On the 27th of October a justice of the peace for Metcalfe wrote from Annotto Bay—"There are several cases of cutting and wounding and other offences brought to my notice, and the civil power cannot deal with them at present." (Minutes of Evidence, p. 1,000.) "There is reason to suspect that a spirit of disaffection prevails in St. Mary's, although, I believe, there have been no overt instances to indicate it. Several persons have been brought up charged with seditious conduct. One man, by sentence of court-martial, received fifty lashes, and another will be forwarded to Buff Bay, to be dealt with by the military authorities there." (Minutes of Evidence, p. 1,000.) On the 30th of October the senior magistrate of Hanover wrote again in pressing terms, enclosing a letter, picked up, threatening to burn down the town, and stating that a war would break out and that all the people in the interior were ready. (Minutes of Evidence, p. 1,002.) And on the 31st the Hon. S. Rennall wrote to say that "a local preacher there was implicated in the rebellion, and that until his apprehension every class of the inhabitants were apparently not secure that the rebellion would not extend to their district; there was, then, no certainty that it would not do so." (Minutes of Evidence, p. 1,004.) These communications were admitted in evidence to show the condition of the island about the 30th, the date of the declaration of amnesty, before stating which it is necessary also to mention a correspondence which passed about this time between the Governor and the Commander-in-chief as to the distribution of the military reinforcements which had just arrived. The Governor, who, it will be seen, was beset with applications for troops and alarms and apprehensions of renewed outbreaks of insurrection, wanted the reinforcements to be disposed of by distribution through the chief districts, and on the 27th of October wrote to the Commander-in-chief to that effect. thinking the reinforcements had arrived, which, however, turned out to be an error, they not arriving until the end of the month, when he wrote again to the like effect. Mr. Eyre stated in these letters :—"We have abundant proof that the same spirit of disaffection and disloyalty which led to the rebellion in St. Thomas-in-the-East exists to a considerable extent in every parish in the island ; and in a country so extensive as Jamaica, and affording so few facilities for receiving early intelligence or for making rapid movements by land, it is absolutely essential that for some time to come a considerable number of points should be occupied as military positions around the coast." (Min. of Evid., p. 1,000.) And again he wrote that advices had reached him from the Custos of St. Anne's which led him to believe that the spirit of disloyalty and sedition were rampant there, that the most threatening language was openly indulged in, and that there was an intention to rise in insurrection about the 2nd of November next, unless timely measures were taken to prevent it. (Minutes of Evidence, p. 1,001.) On the 28th of October, however, the Commander-in-chief wrote to the Governor that he was unable to furnish any detachments from the newly-armed force, and that he greatly feared that the health of the troops would suffer if not in a measure relieved from the arduous work of the last two or three weeks. (Ibid., p. 1,001.) And next day the Commander-in-chief wrote to say that although fresh reinforcements had arrived, he thought it best to concentrate them at head-quarters at Falmouth, instead of breaking them up into detachments, as Mr. Eyre had desired. (Ibid.) The same day the Governor wrote urgently to the Commander-in-chief to desire him to carry out that arrangement. (Ibid., p, 1,002.)

On the 30th October, the proclamation of amnesty thus recited:—

"That through the energy and zeal of our civil, military, and naval forces, the wicked rebellion lately existing in certain parts of the county of Surrey has been subdued, and that the chief instigators thereof and actors therein have been visited with the punishment due to their heinous offences; and whereas we are certified that the inhabitants of the district lately in rebellion are desirous to return to their allegiance."

And then it proceeded to proclaim a pardon to all who should at once come in and submit themselves to the royal authority, except those guilty of arson and murder. (Minutes of Evidence, p. 87.)

Mr. Eyre, in his first examination (put in evidence), thus briefly stated his reasons for continuing martial law for nearly a fortnight afterwards:—

Because there were still a large number of rebels in custody who had not been dealt with, and because there were apprehensions of serious disturbances in other districts; and it was considered necessary that summary punishments should take place with regard to those in custody and those who should be captured, not coming in under the amnesty, before the 13th of November, when the period for which martial law was declared would terminate. (Minutes of Evidence, p. 88.) And he stated that he received communications at this time from almost every part of the island, showing that there were apprehensions of risings. (Ibid.) They were, he said, very numerous, and disclosing a number of little facts, circumstances, and incidents tending to show a seditious spirit and a desire to join a rebellion if an opportunity offered—all indicatory that the country was in a very unsettled state and in a very precarious position. (Ibid.) A vast number of these he afterwards put in, and many were admitted by the magistrate in evidence. Mr. Eyre said on this point in his third examination, "The Commissioners are aware of the steps taken after the proclamation of martial law, that those steps were successful, and that I found myself in a position to proclaim, on the 30th of October, a general amnesty to all persons in the district where the rebellion had existed, excepting only certain persons who were specially excluded." The object of the Government in proclaiming an amnesty thus early, was to offer an opportunity to those who had been in rebellion, but who had not been guilty of the serious crimes of murder and arson, to return to their allegiance. It was not intended to stop the operation of martial law, which would, without any further action on the part of the Government, continue to the 13th of November by the law under which it had been called into existence. The Government did not consider the disturbed districts in a state to admit of martial law being suddenly dispensed with, while the reports received from all parts of the island occasioned such great anxiety for the safety of other districts which were then unprotected as to make it a matter of essential policy to continue martial law until the Government could complete such arrangements as would justify a reasonable hope that the public peace, and the safety of life and property, would not further be seriously endangered. (Minutes of Evidence, p. 991.) Mr. Eyre then proceeded to state the circumstances brought to the notice of the Government, many of which it has been seen were admitted by the magistrate in evidence (though many were, for some reason not very apparent, rejected), and these have been already mentioned. On the 2nd of November Mr. Eyre wrote to the Secretary of State a despatch, in which he reported that he had deemed it expedient to proclaim an amnesty, and proceeded thus:—

"This step will, I have no doubt, lead to the immediate restoration of most of the plunder taken from the houses sacked by the rebels, and to the return of the peasantry to labour on the estates. The districts lately in open rebellion I consider, therefore, now perfectly quieted and safe; indeed, far safer than any other part of the island. The retribution has been so prompt and terrible that it is never likely to be forgotten. The accounts from other parts of the island continue to cause me much anxiety. No actual outbreak has taken place, and I hope none will, but it is manifest that the seeds of sedition and rebellion have been sown broadcast through the land, and that in every parish there are many prepared, if a fitting opportunity offered, to act just as the negroes did in the eastern parishes. In many parts of the country a sympathy with the eastern rebels, and expressions of a desire or intention to do the same in their own parishes, have been publicly indulged in, while the local authorities, from the absence of any organized force to resist a rising, have not been in a position to take up and punish such disloyal language and threats. Since the arrival of troops from Barbadoes I have been enabled to direct such a disposition of the troops as will, if carried out by the military authorities, enable the executive to keep under control and check nearly every parish in the island ; and if it is not practicable in all cases to prevent a rising, we shall be in a position to put it down without much difficulty, as well as to prevent its rapid extension to other parishes, as occurred in St. Thomas-in-the East. There can be no doubt that there has been an intercommunication between the negroes of the different parishes, and an intention to act in concert for the destruction of the white and coloured inhabitants, as is proved by the many remarks and speeches which have reached us in all directions, some of them intimating a knowledge that something was about to occur at St. Thomas-in-the-East, and that they were waiting in other parishes to be guided by the action taken there. There does not appear, however, to have been any actually organized combination to act simultaneously, or if there was it was frustrated by the rising taking place prematurely at Morant Bay. I believe that the military arrangements stated in my letters to General O'Connor (*vide ante*) will render the island secure and restore public confidence." (Minutes of Evidence, p. 1,006.)

It did not appear, however, that these military arrangements were carried out before the 10th of November, and on that day —

"Depositions were sent to the Governor from Falmouth, as to seditious language by negroes about drinking the white man's blood," &c. (Ibid.)

This was the latest of the communications put in before the 13th of November, when martial law terminated.

Various letters of Mr. Eyre were put in evidence on the part of the prosecution to prove his personal direction or sanction of the continued execution of martial law between the 24th of October and the 14th of November, when it terminated.

There was a letter of Mr. Eyre on the 26th of October, directing the three prisoners, Bruce, Phillips, and Levine, to be sent to Morant Bay to be tried. (Papers on Disturbances, p. 99.) So on the 31st of October, 1865, stating that he had directed the Custos in Kingston to examine into and arrange what cases should be sent for trial to Morant Bay, and to send the prisoners down :—

" The Custos of Kingston and another gentleman engaged in examining into the evidence, and arranging the cases against the prisoners (named in accompanying list, and including one Samuel Clarke, who was afterwards executed), came to inform me that the evidence was now complete, except as regards one or two, whom it would be necessary to send to Morant Bay, where further evidence is procurable. I enclose a packet containing the statement of the evidence against the prisoners, addressed to General Nelson." (Ibid., 102.)

Then, on the 2nd of November, after the amnesty :—

"I have to inform you that martial law will cease on the 13th of November, by the operation of the law under which it is called into existence. It will be necessary that all prisoners to be dealt with by martial law should be delivered, either at Morant Bay or at Port Royal, not later than the 11th of November."

On the other hand, certain communications were put in evidence to show that in allowing the continuance of martial law after the amnesty Mr. Eyre acted on the apprehension of imminent danger still impending over the colony.

A letter from Mr. Eyre to Captain Horsey, dated the 23rd of October, representing the imminent occurrence of an outbreak. (Papers on Disturbances, 98.) He stated also in his evidence "there were apprehensions of serious disturbances in other districts, and that it was therefore considered necessary that summary punishment of the rebels still in custody should take place." (Evidence, p. 88.) "That there was a seditious spirit and a desire to form a rebellion, and that the country was in a precarious position." (Ibid.)

He supported this view by producing a number of communications he received between the 30th of October and the 14th of November, *i.e.*, between the amnesty and the cessation of martial law, dwelling strongly also upon this, that the reinforcements had only arrived in the island about the 30th, and that there was great difficulty in their distribution.

The fresh troops, he said, only arrived at the end of October, and were only distributed between that date and the 10th of November. He pointed out that the troops, small as their number was, had to occupy a tract of country comprising 700 or 800 square miles (Evidence, p. 90), and that the country was a very difficult, mountainous country, and it was the rainy season, which caused great difficulty in communication, and consequently would interpose great difficulty in suppressing any further outbreak. That it was the rainy season, and that there was this difficulty of communication. This it had also been stated in the evidence for the prosecution.

II.—THE INDICTMENT.*

MIDDLESEX TO WIT.—The Jurors for our Lady the Queen, upon their oath present that heretofore, to wit, in the 11th and 12th years of the reign of his late Majesty King William the Third, an Act of Parliament was made and passed for the purpose of hearing and determining, in the Court of King's Bench, in England, any oppressions, crimes, and offences, done and committed after the 1st day of August, 1700, by any governor, lieutenant-governor, deputy-governor, or commander-in-chief, of any plantation or colony within his then Majesty's dominions beyond the seas; and that the said Act of Parliament was intituled, "An Act to punish governors of plantations in this kingdom for crimes by them committed in the plantations." And the jurors aforesaid, upon their oath aforesaid, do further present that heretofore, to wit, on the 22nd day of June, 1802, in the 42nd year of the reign of his late Majesty King George the Third, an Act of Parliament was made and passed for the purpose of extending the provisions of the said Act of Parliament so made and passed in the 11th and 12th years of the reign of his late Majesty King William the Third; and that the said Act of Parliament so made and passed in the 42nd year of the reign of his late Majesty King George the Third, was intituled, "An Act for the trying and

---

* It must be borne in mind that this Indictment had been prepared with great care by experienced counsel, after the *lapse of two years* from the Report of a Royal Commission on the case; so that it embraced every possible charge that could be devised against a Governor in respect to the exercise of martial law; and further, that *every charge was negatived on oath.*

punishing in Great Britain persons holding public employments for offences committed abroad." And the jurors aforesaid, upon their oath aforesaid, do further present that on the 13th day of October, 1865 (and long before), Edward John Eyre was a person employed in the service of her present Majesty Queen Victoria in a civil and military station out of Great Britain, to wit, in the Island of Jamaica, and that the said Edward John Eyre being so employed as aforesaid, and whilst he was so employed as aforesaid, unlawfully intending to aggrieve and oppress divers subjects of her said Majesty, in the said Island of Jamaica, within his said command, on the said 13th day of October, in the year aforesaid, at Headquarter House, in the city of Kingston, in the said Island of Jamaica, to wit, in the county of Middlesex, under colour of his said station, unlawfully and oppressively did make and issue a certain illegal and oppressive proclamation, which said proclamation was in the words and figures following, that is to say :—

"Jamaica, S. S.

"Victoria, by the grace of God of the United Kingdom of Great Britain and Ireland, Queen, and of Jamaica, Supreme Lady, Defender of the Faith.

"To all our loving subjects:

"Whereas we are certified of the committal of grievous trespasses and felonies within the parish of St. Thomas-in-the-East, of this our Island of Jamaica, and have reason for expecting that the same may be extended to the neighbouring parishes of the county of Surrey, of our said island, we do hereby, by the authority to us committed by the laws of this our island, declare and announce to all whom it may concern, that martial law shall prevail throughout the said county of Surrey, except in the city and parish of Kingston, and that our military forces shall have all power of exercising the rights of belligerents against such of the inhabitants of the said county, except as aforesaid, as our military forces may consider opposed to our Government and the well-being of our loving subjects.

"Given at Head-quarter House, Kingston, on the 13th day of October, 1865, and in the 29th year of our reign.

"Witness his Excellency, Edward John Eyre, Esq., Captain-General and Governor-in-Chief in and over our said Island of Jamaica and other the territories thereon depending in America, Governor and Commander-in-chief of the colony of British Honduras, Chancellor of our said Island of Jamaica, and Vice-Admiral of the same.

"E. EYRE.

"By his Excellency's command,
"EDWARD JORDAN, Governor's Secretary."

In manifest violation of the liberties of her Majesty's said subjects, to the great perversion of public justice, and against the peace of our said Lady the Queen, her crown and dignity.

2nd Count.—And the jurors aforesaid, upon their oath aforesaid, do further present, that after the making and passing of the said several Acts of Parliament in the first Count of this Indictment mentioned, the said Edward John Eyre was Captain-General and Governor-in-chief in and over a certain colony within her Majesty's dominions beyond the seas, to wit, the Island of Jamaica; and that whilst the said Edward John Eyre was such Governor as aforesaid, to wit, on the 14th day of October, 1865, and on divers other days between the day last mentioned and the 13th day of November in the same year, the said Edward John Eyre, so being such Governor as aforesaid, did unlawfully and oppressively cause and procure the said illegal and oppressive proclamation in the said 1st Count mentioned and set forth to be published and maintained in full force and effect within the county of Surrey, in the said Island of Jamaica, except the city and parish of Kingston, in the said island as aforesaid, for a long space of time, to wit, thirty days, to the great perversion of public justice, to the great damage of all the liege subjects of our said Lady the Queen, within the said island, and against the peace of our said Lady the Queen, her crown and dignity.

3rd Count.—And the jurors aforesaid, upon their oath aforesaid, do further present, that after the making and passing of the said several Acts of Parliament in the 1st Count of this Indictment mentioned, the said Edward John Eyre was Captain-General and Governor-in-chief in and over a certain colony within her Majesty's dominions beyond the seas, to wit, the Island of Jamaica; and that whilst the said Edward John Eyre was such Governor as aforesaid, to wit, on the 14th day of October, 1865, and on divers other days between that day and the 13th day of November in the year aforesaid, certain pretended and unlawful courts-martial assembled in divers parts of the county of Surrey, in the said Island of Jamaica, not being within the parish and city of Kingston, in the said island, and that certain unlawful and pretended courts-martial, so assembled as aforesaid, proceeded to hear and determine divers grave charges against divers liege subjects of our said Lady the Queen, and that the said unlawful and pretended courts-martial so assembled as aforesaid proceeded to adjudge and sentence divers liege subjects of our said Lady the Queen to divers cruel and unlawful punishments, to wit, flogging and imprisonment. And the jurors aforesaid, upon their oath aforesaid, do further present, that on the said 14th day of October in the year aforesaid, and on divers other days between the said day last mentioned and the 13th day of

November in the year aforesaid, the said John Edward Eyre had full knowledge and notice of the said unlawful acts of the said pretended courts-martial as aforesaid; and it became and was the duty of the said Edward John Eyre, as such Governor as aforesaid, to prohibit and prevent the carrying out of the said sentences of the said pretended courts-martial and the infliction of the said unlawful punishments; and that during all the time aforesaid the said Edward John Eyre had full authority and power, as such Governor as aforesaid, to prohibit and prevent the said carrying out of the sentences aforesaid, and the said inflictions of the unlawful punishments aforesaid; and that the said Edward John Eyre unlawfully then and there, to wit, in the county of Middlesex, during all the times aforesaid, so being such Governor as aforesaid, and so having authority and power as aforesaid, did not and would not prohibit and prevent the carrying out of the said illegal sentences as aforesaid, and the said unlawful punishments as aforesaid, but wholly neglected and refused so to do, contrary to his said duty as such Governor as aforesaid, to the great damage of divers liege subjects of our said Lady the Queen, as aforesaid, and against the peace of our said Lady the Queen, her crown and dignity.

4th Count.—And the jurors aforesaid, upon their oath aforesaid, do further present that, after the making and passing of the said several Acts of Parliament, in the 1st Count of this Indictment mentioned, to wit, on the 13th day of October in the year aforesaid, to wit, in the county of Middlesex, the said Edward John Eyre then being Captain-General and Governor-in-chief in and over a certain colony within her Majesty's dominions beyond the seas, to wit, the Island of Jamaica, did, in the exercise of his said office, make and issue a certain proclamation, and which said proclamation was and is in the words and figures following, that is to say:—

"Jamaica, S. S.

"Victoria, by the grace of God of the United Kingdom of Great Britain and Ireland, Queen, and of Jamaica, Supreme Lady, Defender of the Faith.

"To all our loving subjects:

"Whereas we are certified of the committal of grievous trespasses and felonies within the parish of St. Thomas-in-the-East, of this our Island of Jamaica, and have reason for expecting that the same may be extended to the neighbouring parishes of the county of Surrey, of our said island, we do hereby, by the authority to us committed by the laws of this our island, declare and announce to all whom it may concern, that martial law shall prevail throughout the said county of Surrey, except in the city and parish of Kingston, and that our military forces shall have all power of exercising the rights of belligerents against such of the inhabitants of the said county, except as aforesaid, as our military forces may consider opposed to our Government and the well-being of our loving subjects.

"Given at Head-quarter House, Kingston, on the 13th of October, 1865, and in the 29th year of our reign.

"Witness his Excellency, Edward John Eyre, Esq., Captain-General and Governor-in-chief in and over our said Island of Jamaica and other the territories thereon depending in America, Governor and Commander-in-chief of the colony of British Honduras, Chancellor of our said Island of Jamaica, and Vice-Admiral of the same.

"E. EYRE.
"By his Excellency's command,
"EDWARD JORDAN, Governor's Secretary."

And the jurors aforesaid, upon their oath aforesaid, do further present, that the said Edward John Eyre, in pursuance of and under and by virtue of the said proclamation, did declare that martial law should prevail throughout the said county of Surrey, in the said proclamation mentioned, except in the city and parish of Kingston therein mentioned, and did profess to empower the military forces of our said Lady the Queen, then and there being, to exercise the rights of belligerents against such of the inhabitants of the said county, except as therein and hereinbefore mentioned, as the said military forces might consider opposed to the Government of our said Lady the Queen and the well-being of her subjects. And the jurors aforesaid, upon their oath aforesaid, do further present, that the said Edward John Eyre, then and there being such Governor as aforesaid, and whilst he was such Governor as aforesaid, to wit, on the 17th day of October, in the year aforesaid, to wit, in the county of Middlesex, unlawfully, oppressively, and without any lawful or reasonable authority whatsoever, and under the false colour and pretence of acting under and in accordance with the said proclamation, and under and by virtue of the laws then and there in force, did cause and procure one George William Gordon to be taken into custody and imprisoned for a long space of time, to wit, for two hours, at a certain place not being within the district within which martial law had so been declared and proclaimed; but on the contrary, in a certain place excepted from the operation of the said proclamation and the said martial law, to wit, in the parish of Kingston aforesaid; and that the said Edward John Eyre so then being such Governor as aforesaid, and whilst he was such Governor afterwards, to wit, on the 18th day of October in the year aforesaid, unlawfully, oppressively, and without any lawful or reasonable authority whatsoever, and under the false colour and pretence of acting under and in accordance with the said proclamation, and under and by virtue of the laws then and there in force, did cause and procure the said George William Gordon to be unlawfully and forcibly removed and conveyed from and out of the said parish of Kingston, where he then was, into and upon a certain ship called the "Wolverine," and unlawfully and oppressively did cause the said George William Gordon to be unlawfully kept, detained, and imprisoned on board the said ship for a long space of time, to wit, for three days, and to be unlawfully, wrongfully, and oppressively, without any lawful authority in that behalf, carried on board the said ship from the said parish of Kingston, to a certain place called Morant Bay, in the parish of St. Thomas-in-the-East, in the said Island of Jamaica; and that the said Edward John Eyre, so then being such Governor as aforesaid, and whilst he was such Governor afterwards, to wit, on the 20th day of October in the year aforesaid, unlawfully, oppressively, and without any lawful or reasonable authority whatsoever, and under the false colour and pretence of acting under and in accordance with the said proclamation, and under and by virtue of the laws then and there in force, did cause and procure the said George William Gordon to be unlawfully and forcibly removed and conveyed from and out of the said ship called the "Wolverine," where he then was, and to be delivered into the custody of one Alexander Abercrombie Nelson, then acting as Brigadier-General in command of certain military forces of our said Lady the Queen, at Morant Bay aforesaid, and to be imprisoned at Morant Bay aforesaid, and to be kept and detained so imprisoned for a long space of time, to wit, for three days, to the great injury, oppression, and damage of the said George William Gordon, and against the peace of our said Lady the Queen, her crown and dignity.

5th Count.—And the jurors aforesaid, upon their oath aforesaid, do further present, that the said Edward John Eyre being so employed in such station as aforesaid, unlawfully intending to injure, prejudice, and oppress one George William Gordon, then being in the said parish and city of Kingston, afterwards and whilst he was so employed as aforesaid, to wit, on the 17th day of October, 1865, to wit, in the county of Middlesex, unlawfully, oppressively, and without any reasonable or lawful cause whatsoever, under colour of his said station, did cause and procure the said George William Gordon to be taken into custody and imprisoned, and to be kept and detained so imprisoned for a long space of time, to wit, for two hours, in the said parish and city of Kingston, in the said Island of Jamaica, and other wrongs to the said George William Gordon then and there did, to the great injury, oppression, and damage of the said George William Gordon, and against the peace of our said Lady the Queen, her crown and dignity.

6th Count.—And the jurors aforesaid, upon their oath aforesaid, do further present, that the said Edward John Eyre being so employed in such station as aforesaid, and whilst he was so employed as aforesaid, unlawfully intending to injure, prejudice, and oppress one George William Gordon, afterwards, to wit, on the 18th day of October, 1865, to wit, in the county of Middlesex, unlawfully, oppressively, and without any reasonable or lawful cause whatsoever, under colour of his said station, did cause and procure the said George William Gordon to be forcibly removed and conveyed from and out of the said parish and city of Kingston, where he then was, into and upon a certain ship, to wit, her Majesty's ship "Wolverine," and there to be imprisoned and to be kept and detained so imprisoned for a long space of time, to wit, for three days, and to be carried in the said ship from the said parish and city of Kingston to Morant Bay, in the parish of St. Thomas-in-the-East, in the said Island of Jamaica, and other wrongs to the said George William Gordon then and there did, to the great injury, oppression, and damage of the said George William Gordon, and against the peace of our said Lady the Queen, her crown and dignity.

7th Count.—And the jurors aforesaid, upon their oath aforesaid, do further present, that the said Edward John Eyre being so employed in such station as aforesaid, and whilst he was so employed as aforesaid, unlawfully intending to injure, prejudice, and oppress one George William Gordon, afterwards, to wit, on the 20th October, 1865, to wit, in the county of Middlesex, unlawfully and oppressively, under colour of his said station, did cause and procure the said George William Gordon to be forcibly removed and conveyed from and out of her Majesty's ship "Wolverine," into the custody of one Alexander Abercrombie Nelson, then acting as Brigadier-General in command of certain military forces at Morant Bay, in the said Island of Jamaica, and to be imprisoned at Morant Bay aforesaid, and to be kept and detained so imprisoned for a long space of time, to wit, for three days, and other wrongs to the said George William Gordon then and there did, to the great injury, oppression, and damage of the said George William Gordon, and against the peace of our said Lady the Queen, her crown and dignity.

8th Count.—And the jurors aforesaid, upon their oath aforesaid, do further present, that the said Edward John Eyre being so employed in such station as aforesaid, and whilst he was so employed as aforesaid, unlawfully intending to injure, prejudice, and oppress one George William Gordon, afterwards, to wit, on the 21st day of October, 1865, to wit, in the county of Middlesex, unlawfully and oppressively, under colour of his said station, did cause and procure the said George William Gordon to be taken in custody before a certain illegal and oppressive tribunal, to wit, a pretended court-martial composed of two officers of her Majesty's naval service and one officer of her Majesty's army, there and then to defend himself upon certain grave charges, to wit, high treason and rebellion against our said Lady the Queen ; and that the said pretended tribunal did hold a pretended court, and did conduct the proceedings before the same in contravention of the laws then and there in force, and of the rules of natural justice, and did find the said George William Gordon to be guilty of the charges aforesaid, and did adjudge the said George William Gordon to suffer certain punishment; and that the said Edward John Eyre, well knowing the premises, and being such Governor as aforesaid, did unlawfully authorise, approve, ratify, and sanction the said unlawful and oppressive acts then and there done and committed by the said illegal tribunal, to the great injury, oppression, and damage of the said George William Gordon and against the peace of our said Lady the Queen, her crown, and dignity.

9th Count.—And the jurors aforesaid, upon their oath aforesaid, do further present, that the said Edward John Eyre, being so employed in such station as aforesaid, and whilst he was so employed aforesaid afterwards, to wit, on the 23rd day of October, 1865, to wit, in the county of Middlesex, unlawfully and oppressively and intending to injure one Robert George Bruce, did cause and procure the said Robert George Bruce to be taken into custody at a certain place, to wit, Vere, in the county of Middlesex, in the said Island of Jamaica, which said place was not within the district within which martial law had been declared and proclaimed, under the colour and pretence of the said proclamation in the first count set forth, and unlawfully did cause and procure the said Robert George Bruce, so being in such unproclaimed place as aforesaid, to be forcibly removed and conveyed from and out of the said place into a certain other place, to wit, Morant Bay, in the said county of Surrey, in the said Island of Jamaica, which said other place was within the district within which martial law had been declared and proclaimed, under the colour and pretence of the said proclamation as aforesaid, and there to be delivered into the custody of certain officers and soldiers, and there to be unlawfully imprisoned and detained for a long space of time, to wit, for fifty-five days, and other wrongs to the said Robert George Bruce then and there did, to the great injury, oppression, and damage of the said Robert George Bruce and against the peace of our said Lady the Queen, her crown and dignity.

10th Count.—And the jurors aforesaid, upon their oath aforesaid, do further present, that the said Edward John Eyre, so being such Governor as aforesaid, and so being employed as aforesaid afterwards, and whilst he was such Governor, and whilst he was so employed, to wit, on the 23rd day of October in the year aforesaid, in and upon one Robert George Bruce, in the peace of God and our said Lady the Queen, then and there being unlawfully and under colour of his said office and employment, did make an assault, and him the said Robert George Bruce falsely, unlawfully, oppressively, and against the will of the said Robert George Bruce, and against the laws then and there in force, and without any legal warrant or authority, did imprison and detain for the space of sixty days, and other wrongs to the said Robert George Bruce then and there did, to the great damage of the said Robert George Bruce and against the peace of our said Lady the Queen, her crown and dignity.

11th Count.—And the jurors aforesaid, upon their oath aforesaid, do further present, that the said Edward John Eyre, being so employed in such station as aforesaid, and whilst he was so employed as aforesaid afterwards, to wit, on the 23rd day of October, 1865, to wit, in the county of Middlesex, unlawfully and oppressively, and intending to injure one Alexander Phillips, did cause and procure the said Alexander Phillips to be taken into custody at a certain place, to wit, Vere, in the county of Middlesex, in the said Island of Jamaica, which said place was not within the district within which martial law had been declared and proclaimed, under the colour and pretence of the said proclamation in the first count of this indictment

set forth, and unlawfully did cause and procure the said
Alexander Phillips, so being in such unproclaimed place as
aforesaid, to be forcibly removed and conveyed from and
out of the said place into a certain other place, to wit,
Morant Bay, in the said Island of Jamaica, which said
other place was within the district within which martial
law had been declared and proclaimed, under the colour
and pretence of the said proclamation as aforesaid, and
there to be delivered into the custody of certain officers and
soldiers, and there to be unlawfully imprisoned and detained
for a long space of time, to wit, for eight days, and other
wrongs to the said Alexander Phillips then and there did,
to the great injury, oppression, and damage of the said
Alexander Phillips and against the peace of our said Lady
the Queen, her crown and dignity.

12*th Count.*—And the jurors aforesaid, upon their oath
aforesaid, do further present, that the said Edward John
Eyre, so being such Governor as aforesaid, and so being
employed as aforesaid afterwards, and whilst he was such
Governor, and whilst he was so employed as aforesaid, to
wit, on the 23rd day of October in the year aforesaid, in
and upon Alexander Phillips, in the peace of God and our
said Lady the Queen, then and there being unlawfully and
under colour of his said office and employment, did make
an assault, and him the said Alexander Phillips falsely,
unlawfully, and oppressively, and against the will of the
said Alexander Phillips, and against the laws then and
there in force, and without any legal warrant or authority,
did imprison and detain for the space of twelve days, and
other wrongs to the said Alexander Phillips then and
there did, to the great damage of the said Alexander Phillips and against the peace of our said Lady the Queen, her
crown and dignity.

13*th Count.*—And the jurors aforesaid, upon their oath
aforesaid, do further present, that the said Edward John
Eyre, whilst he was such Governor, and whilst he was so

employed as aforesaid, to wit, on the 4th day of November in the year aforesaid, in and upon the said Alexander Phillips, unlawfully and oppressively, and under colour of his said office and employment, did make an assault, and him the said Alexander Phillips did beat, flog, wound, and ill-treat, and other wrongs to the said Alexander Phillips then and there did, to the great damage of the said Alexander Phillips, and against the peace of our said Lady the Queen, her crown and dignity.

14th Count.—And the jurors aforesaid, upon their oath aforesaid, do further present, that the said Edward John Eyre, being so employed in such station as aforesaid, and whilst he was so employed as aforesaid afterwards, to wit, on the 23rd day of October, 1865, to wit, in the county of Middlesex, unlawfully and oppressively, and intending to injure one Benjamin Morris, did cause and procure the said Benjamin Morris to be taken into custody at a certain place, to wit, Vere, in the county of Middlesex, in the said Island of Jamaica, which said place was not within the district within which martial law had been declared and proclaimed, under the colour and pretence of the said proclamation in the first count of this indictment set forth, and unlawfully did cause and procure the said Benjamin Morris, so being in such unproclaimed place as aforesaid, to be forcibly removed and conveyed from and out of the said place to a certain other place, to wit, Morant Bay, in the said county of Surrey, in the said Island of Jamaica, which said other place was within the district within which martial law had been declared and proclaimed, under the colour and pretence of the said proclamation as aforesaid, and there to be delivered into the custody of certain officers and soldiers, and there to be unlawfully imprisoned and detained for a long space of time, to wit, for eight days, and other wrongs to the said Benjamin Morris then and there did, to the great injury, oppression, and damage of the said

Benjamin Morris, and against the peace of our said Lady
the Queen, her crown and dignity.

15th Count.—And the jurors aforesaid, upon their oath
aforesaid, do further present, that the said Edward John
Eyre, whilst he was such Governor as aforesaid, and whilst
he was so employed as aforesaid afterwards, to wit, on the
23rd day of October, in the year aforesaid, under colour
of his said office and employment, in and upon Benjamin
Morris, in the peace of God and our said Lady the Queen,
then and there being unlawfully, did make an assault, and
him the said Benjamin Morris falsely, unlawfully, oppressively, and against the will of the said Benjamin Morris,
against the laws then and there in force, and without any
legal warrant or authority, did imprison and detain for
the space of twelve days, and other wrongs to the said Benjamin Morris then did, to the great damage of the said
Benjamin Morris, and against the peace of our said Lady
the Queen, her crown and dignity.

16th Count.—And the jurors aforesaid, upon their oath
aforesaid, do further present that the said Edward John
Eyre, whilst he was such Governor as aforesaid, and whilst
he was so employed as aforesaid afterwards, to wit, on the
4th day of November, in the year aforesaid, under colour
of his said office and employment, in and upon the said
Benjamin Morris unlawfully and oppressively did make
an assault, and him the said Benjamin Morris unlawfully
did beat, flog, wound, and ill-treat, and other wrongs to
the said Benjamin Morris then and there did, to the great
damage of the said Benjamin Morris, and against the peace
of our said Lady the Queen, her crown and dignity.

17th Count.—And the jurors aforesaid, upon their oath
aforesaid, do further present that the said Edward John
Eyre, being so employed in such station as aforesaid, and
whilst he was so employed as aforesaid afterwards, to wit,
on the 21st day of October, 1865, to wit, in the county

of Middlesex, unlawfully and oppressively, and intending to injure one Frederick Augustus Burt Vinen, did cause and procure the said Frederick Augustus Burt Vinen to be taken into custody at a certain place, to wit, Kingston, in the said county of Surrey, in the said Island of Jamaica, which said place was not within the district within which martial law had been declared and proclaimed, under the colour and pretence of the said proclamation in the first count of this indictment set forth, and unlawfully did cause and procure the said Frederick Augustus Burt Vinen, so being in such unproclaimed place as aforesaid, to be forcibly removed and conveyed from and out of the said place into a certain other place, to wit, Up Park Camp, in the said county of Surrey, in the said Island of Jamaica, which said other place was within the district within which martial law had been declared and proclaimed, under the colour and pretence of the said proclamation as aforesaid, and there to be delivered into the custody of certain officers and soldiers, and there to be unlawfully imprisoned and detained for a long space of time, to wit, for twenty-one days, and other wrongs to the said Frederick Augustus Burt Vinen then and there did, to the great injury, oppression, and damage of the said Frederick Augustus Burt Vinen, and against the peace of our said Lady the Queen, her crown and dignity.

18*th Count.*—And the jurors aforesaid, upon their oath aforesaid, do further present, that the said Edward John Eyre, whilst he was such Governor as aforesaid, and whilst he was so employed as aforesaid, to wit, on the 21st day of October, in the year aforesaid, under colour of his said office and employment, in and upon Frederick Augustus Burt Vinen, in the peace of God and our said Lady the Queen, then and there being, unlawfully did make an assault, and him the said Frederick Augustus Burt Vinen falsely, unlawfully, oppressively, and against the will of the said Frederick Augustus Burt Vinen, and against the laws then and there in force, and without any legal warrant or authority, did imprison and detain for the space of twenty-one days, and other wrongs to the said Frederick Augustus Burt Vinen then did, to the great damage of the said Frederick Augustus Burt Vinen, and against the peace of our said Lady the Queen, her crown and dignity.

19th Count.—And the jurors aforesaid, upon their oath aforesaid, do further present, that the said Edward John Eyre being so employed in such station as aforesaid, and whilst he was so employed as aforesaid afterwards, to wit, on the 1st day of November, 1865, to wit, in the county of Middlesex, unlawfully and oppressively, and intending to injure one Sidney Levien, did cause and procure the said Sidney Levien to be taken into custody at a certain place, to wit, Montego Bay, in the county of Cornwall, in the said Island of Jamaica, which said place was not within the district within which martial law had been declared and proclaimed, under the colour and pretence of the said proclamation in the 1st count of this indictment set forth, and unlawfully did cause and procure the said Sidney Levien, so being in such unproclaimed place as aforesaid, to be forcibly removed and conveyed from and out of the said place into a certain other place, to wit, Morant Bay, in the said county of Surrey, in the said Island of Jamaica, which said other place was within the district within which martial law had been declared and proclaimed, under the colour and pretence of the said proclamation as aforesaid, and there to be delivered into the custody of certain officers and soldiers, and there to be unlawfully imprisoned and detained for a long space of time, to wit, for thirty-six days, and other wrongs to the said Sidney Levien then and there did, to the great injury, oppression, and damage of the said Sidney Levien, and against the peace of our said Lady the Queen, her crown and dignity.

20th Count.—And the jurors aforesaid, upon their oath aforesaid, do further present, that the said Edward John

E

Eyre, whilst he was such Governor as aforesaid, and whilst he was so employed as aforesaid, to wit, on the 1st day of November in the year aforesaid, under colour of his said office and employment, in and upon Sidney Levien, in the peace of God and our said Lady the Queen, then and there being, unlawfully did make an assault, and him the said Sidney Levien falsely, unlawfully, oppressively, and against the will of the said Sidney Levien, and against the laws then and there in force, and without any legal warrant or authority, did imprison and detain for the space of thirty-eight days, and other wrongs to the said Sidney Levien then did, to the great damage of the said Sidney Levien, and against the peace of our said Lady the Queen, her crown and dignity.

21*st Count.*—And the jurors aforesaid, upon their oath aforesaid, do further present, that the said Edward John Eyre, at the time of the commission of the offences and misdemeanours in this count hereinafter mentioned, was a person employed in the service of our said Lady the Queen out of Great Britain, and then was Captain-General and Governor-in-chief in and over the Island of Jamaica, and other the territories thereon depending in America, and then was Governor and Commander-in-chief of the colony of British Honduras, and Chancellor of the said Island of Jamaica, and Vice-Admiral of the same. And the jurors aforesaid, upon their oath aforesaid, do further present, that the said Edward John Eyre, not regarding his duty in that behalf, unlawfully and maliciously devising and intending to oppress divers of the liege subjects of our said Lady the Queen, then residing and being in the said Island of Jamaica, did, on the 17th day of October, in the year aforesaid, and on divers other days and times between that day and the 22nd day of December in the year aforesaid, to wit, at Westminster, in the county of Middlesex, unjustly, unlawfully, maliciously, and oppressively, under colour of his said office and employment, and contrary to the laws

of the realm, cause and procure divers of her Majesty's
liege subjects then inhabiting the said island, to wit, one
George William Gordon, one Alexander Phillips, one Benjamin Morris, one Robert George Bruce, one Sidney
Levien, and one Frederick Augustus Burt Vinen, and
divers other persons, to be illegally, and without sufficient
warrant in that behalf, arrested and imprisoned, contrary
to the said laws, and did unlawfully and maliciously,
and under colour of his said office and employment, contrary to the said laws, cause and procure the said George
William Gordon, and divers other persons, to be brought
to trial before a certain unlawful and pretended tribunal
upon certain grave charges, and unlawfully, knowingly,
and oppressively, and contrary to his duty in that behalf,
did sanction by his authority the findings and sentences of
the said unlawful and pretended tribunal upon the trials of
the said persons, and did unlawfully, maliciously, and under
colour of his said office and employment, cause and procure
the said Alexander Phillips and Benjamin Morris to be
falsely imprisoned and detained for many days, and to be
unlawfully flogged, beaten, and punished respectively,
they, the said Alexander Phillips and Benjamin Morris, at
the time they were so flogged, beaten, and punished as
aforesaid, not having been tried for any offence before any
tribunal whatsoever, nor charged with any offence whatsoever, and did unlawfully and maliciously, and under
colour of his said office and employment, and contrary to
the laws then and there in force, cause, procure, and induce
the officers commanding the troops of our said Lady the
Queen, and the said troops then being in the Island of
Jamaica, to treat divers large numbers of the liege subjects
of our said Lady the Queen, then inhabiting the said
Island of Jamaica, as alien enemies, and did cause and procure the said liege subjects as aforesaid to be cruelly
oppressed, wounded, and beaten, and did cause and procure divers houses and other property of divers of the said

liege subjects, situate in the Island of Jamaica, to be burnt and destroyed, without any sufficient cause or justification for the same, and under colour of his said office and employment, did unlawfully, maliciously, and oppressively cause and procure the said Robert George Bruce, Frederick Augustus Burt Vinen, and Sidney Levien, liege subjects of our said Lady the Queen as aforesaid, to be unlawfully imprisoned for a long space of time, to wit, for many days, without the said Robert George Bruce, Frederick Augustus Burt Vinen, and Sidney Levien being brought to trial for any offence, and did cause and procure the said Robert George Bruce and Sidney Levien to be unlawfully and oppressively imprisoned and detained, to wit, in the custody of one Alexander Abercrombie Nelson, for a long space of time after the said Alexander Abercrombie Nelson and others, then being officers of the troops of our said Lady the Queen, had duly certified and made known to the said Edward John Eyre that the said Robert George Bruce and Sidney Levien could not legally be detained by them, to the great damage of the said George William Gordon, the said Alexander Phillips, the said Benjamin Morris, the said Robert George Bruce, the said Sidney Levien, the said Frederick Augustus Burt Vinen, and the said liege subjects of our said Lady the Queen, in contempt of our said Lady the Queen and her laws, in manifest violation of the liberties of the subjects of our said Lady the Queen, to the great perversion of public justice, in breach and violation of the duty of his said office as such Governor and officer as aforesaid, and against the peace of our said Lady the Queen, her crown and dignity.

III.—CHARGE TO THE GRAND JURY.*

Mr. Justice Blackburn :—Gentlemen, you are summoned and empannelled on this occasion as a Grand Jury of the county of Middlesex, in this Court of Queen's Bench, to make inquiry into a case which you have all probably heard a great deal of, the case of Mr. Eyre, late Governor of Jamaica. It will no doubt be proved before you, and will not be disputed, that in the year 1865 Mr. Eyre was Governor of Jamaica, and that, in October of that year, upon the breaking out of an insurrection, Mr. Eyre, as Governor, and in order to put it down, took steps into the legality of which inquiry is now to be made. It is not disputed that he did, with the assent of his council, proclaim martial law, and put it in force—in this sense, I mean, that, for the purpose of putting down the insurrection, he not only caused troops to act in the proclaimed district for the purpose of putting down the insurrection and suppressing armed resistance, but he also caused what is called martial law, in the sense of summary process, superseding the common law, to be put in force; and that a number of persons were tried by this summary process, not by a jury in the ordinary way, and that he caused the sentences to be executed, a very considerable number being capital, and others severe punishments; and further, that he caused this to be done during a period of thirty days, which, by a local Act, to which I shall have to call your attention, was the utmost limit he had power to do. The question is whether, in doing these things, he did anything for which he is criminally responsible.

---

* Delivered 2nd June, 1868. It is printed from the short-hand writer's notes, corrected by the Learned Judge.

I need hardly tell you that it is of very great importance that the law upon this subject should be accurately known; and when I have explained to you what the law is, you will have to consider and decide the questions of fact. It will be your responsibility to decide the facts properly; it is my responsibility to give you, to the best of my ability, a proper guidance as to the law, to enable you to determine the serious matter you will have ultimately to decide. When I have explained what the law is, you will have to decide what you think, applying the law to the facts, ought to be done in this matter.

In the first place, gentlemen, I must explain to you the way in which the case comes before you. By an Act which was passed soon after the Revolution, in the reign of William III., power was given that when the governor of a colony had been guilty of oppressive conduct he might be tried in this country as the king by his commission might appoint. It is not, however, under that Act that we are now acting, but under a subsequent Act, which was passed in the 42nd of George III., Chapter 85, which enacted in substance that if any governor of a colony or any military officer holding any office in a colony—I need not trouble you with any others—should be guilty of any crime, misdemeanour, or offence in the exercise or execution of his office, or under colour of it, he shall be liable to be tried here in the Court of Queen's Bench, the indictment to be found by a Grand Jury of Middlesex here; and if they find the indictment, the case to be tried by a jury of the county of Middlesex, exactly as if the offence had been committed in the county of Middlesex itself. There can be no question whatever that all that Mr. Eyre did was done by him as Governor of Jamaica, and that if there was anything that he did which are crimes, misdemeanours, or offences, they were, no doubt, done in execution or under colour of his office. So the question—and it is a most important question—comes to be whether they are "crimes, misdemeanours, and offences." What is the rule or test of the criminal responsibility for such acts done by a Governor, when acting, as Mr. Eyre undoubtedly was, as Governor, and for the purpose, I think you will not doubt, of putting down an insurrection actually in the colony? I need not tell you that it is a question of very great importance indeed that the law should be distinctly understood,—a question of grave and great importance, not only to Mr. Eyre, but to every one else, to ascertain whether he has been guilty of a crime, or whether he has exceeded his duty in such a way as to make him criminally responsible.

Now, gentlemen, the first question, of course, that arises upon that is, what is the rule of law, where an officer is employed under such circumstances that it is his duty to put down an insurrection; what are the circumstances that will make him criminally responsible? I think that the legal duty, and consequently the legal responsibility of an officer placed in such a situation, when it becomes his duty to suppress the insurrection, varies, and must vary according to the power he has, either by the general law or by particular statutes referring to his particular case. The powers of a governor of a colony, for instance, are different from, and more extensive than, those of a lord-lieutenant of a county of England, or a mayor of a borough in England, in which a riot or insurrection has broken out; and consequently both what he may be authorised to do and what he may be punishable or blameable for if he does not do, is different in his case from theirs, but the principle upon which the responsibility of each officer depends is, I think, the same. The officer is bound to exercise the powers which the law gives him in the manner which, under the circumstances, is right; and if he fails to exercise those powers, if something which he ought to do is not done by him and mischief occurs, then, if the circumstances are such as to make it his duty to exercise them, and he does not do it, he neglects his duty; and if the neglect is such and to such an extent as to amount to criminal negligence, then he is guilty of a crime for which he may be indicted. All this was considered carefully in a case which occurred about thirty years or more ago—I dare say many of you have heard about it—the case at the time of the Reform Bill Riots at Bristol, when, proper steps not being taken to check those riots, they continued for two or three days, and during that time a large portion of Bristol was burnt, and great mischief took place. The Government of the day thought that Mr. Pinney, the then mayor, was responsible for not having exercised his duty as mayor in putting down those riots. That is what we might almost call the converse of the present case. At present the charge against Mr. Eyre is that he exceeded his powers and is criminally responsible for doing too much. In Pinney's case the charge was that he had fallen short of his powers, and did too little, but I consider that the direction of the Court of King's Bench at that time affords a very good guide to me in laying down what I consider the principles of law applicable to the present case. Now in that case the case came on for a trial at bar in this court where a full court sat on the trial; one judge only spoke in addressing the jury, but he conveyed their united opinion upon it. In the book where it is reported it does not give the whole of what occurred, but a very competent and learned reporter, now no more, gives the effect of it. Littledale (Justice) said, "That a party intrusted with the duty of putting down a riot, whether by virtue of an office of his own seeking (as in the ordinary case of a magistrate) or imposed upon him (as that of a constable), is bound to hit the exact line between excess and failure of duty, and that the difficulty of so doing, though it might be some ground for a lenient consideration of his conduct on the part of the jury, was no legal defence to a charge like the present. Nor could a party so charged excuse himself on the mere ground of honest intention. He might omit acting to the extent of his duty from a perfectly good feeling, and that might be considered in apportioning punishment ; but the question for the jury must be whether or not he had done what his duty in point of law required. The subject of inquiry, therefore, in that case would be whether the defendant had done all that he knew was in his power to suppress the riot that could reasonably be expected from a man of honesty and of ordinary prudence, firmness, and activity under the circumstances in which he was placed. Honesty of intention, though not of itself sufficient to exculpate, would form an ingredient in the case to be taken into consideration. The learned judge then stated, as the two points on which the inquiry would turn, whether the Defendant used those means which the law requires to assemble a sufficient force for suppressing the riot and preventing the mischief which occurred; and secondly, whether he had made use of the force which was obtained, and also of his own personal exertion, to prevent mischief, as might reasonably have been expected from a firm and honest man." (The King *v.* Pinney, 3rd Barnwell and Adolphus, King's Bench Reports, page 958.) Then, after commenting on the evidence, he finally leaves it to the jury, upon these two questions, to say whether or not, under the circumstances, there was " criminal negligence," a phrase, I think, which means this. Negligence simply, mere error of judgment in not doing all that he ought to have done, would not be matter which a man would be criminally responsible for; but if he did so far neglect his duty that he ought to have discharged according to the rule there laid down, if he did not do that which a man of reasonable and ordinary firmness would have done under the circumstances, to such a degree that his neglect of duty was criminal, then he should be found guilty, not otherwise. It is a phrase constantly used in criminal cases, but the amount of negligence that would make a man so responsible cannot be defined. It is not a little failure of duty that would make him criminally responsible ; a great failure of duty undoubtedly would. The line between the two is hard to define, and must be left, to a very great extent, in each individual case to the common sense of the jury, whether or not the degree of failure of duty is criminal. That is what I understand to be laid down by the Court of King's Bench at that time in deciding that case.

Now I think where the inquiry is whether an officer is guilty of misdemeanour from an excess beyond his duty, the principle is very much the same, or rather it is the complement of that laid down in the case of Rex v. Pinney. If the officer does some act altogether beyond the power conferred upon him by law, so that it could never under any state of circumstances have been his duty to do it, he is responsible according to the quality of that act; and even if the doing of that illegal act was the salvation of the country, that, though it might be a good ground for the legislature afterwards passing an Act of Indemnity, would be no bar in law to a criminal prosecution; that is, if he has done something clearly beyond his power. But if the act which he has done is one which in a proper state of circumstances the officer was authorised to do, so that in an extreme case, on the principle laid down in R. r. Pinney, he might be criminally punished for failure of duty for not doing it, then the case becomes very different. Honesty of intention in such a case is very important, for if it be shown that the officer, under colour of exercising his office, was really moved by any other motive than an honest desire to do his duty, there is no doubt at all he would be guilty of a misdemeanour; even if there was a perfectly honest intention, that would not of itself conclusively determine the question in the officer's favour, although it would be a very important element indeed. I think the officer is bound under such circumstances to bring to the exercise of his duty ordinary firmness, judgment, and discretion. I think he is bound to do that, and I think in such a case the jury have to determine upon the evidence, first, whether the circumstances were in fact such that what was done really was in excess of the duty of the officer, and secondly, whether a person placed in the position of that officer, having the information that he had, believing what he did believe, and knowing what he did know, if exercising ordinary firmness, judgment, and moderation, would have perceived it was an excess. Much allowance should be made for the difficulty of his position, but not too much, and I think it must ultimately in such a case always be a question of more or less, and therefore a question of fact; and as all questions of fact must be determined by somebody, and the law says they shall be determined by a jury and not by a judge; then it must be a question for a jury whether there was in the particular case so much excess as to amount to a criminal excess.

Now, gentlemen, I have written down the words I was going to use to you, because it is a very important point of law, and I wish to have it accurately laid down, that I may be sure that I have said precisely what I intended. You see two things are to be considered, first, were the acts done by Mr. Eyre in the view that I have been already explaining to you utterly beyond his competence, things that he could never have been bound to do at all. If so, the law would be simple and straight, and I should be obliged to say to you, as I did before, that those acts were totally illegal. There may be a ground for applying for mercy to the Crown or for an Act of Indemnity, but the mere fact of the good intention, or even the benefit that may have been done, would not be a bar to a criminal indictment; but then if all that Mr. Eyre did were acts which he had in his competence to do, supposing the circumstances to be such that it would have been proper to do them; and consequently, according to the case of King *v.* Pinney, he would be bound to do in a proper case, and even would be criminally punishable if he failed to do them, then, in that case the question comes to be what I said before to you,—were the circumstances really such that what he did was in excess of what he ought to have done: and secondly, following upon that, which is not decisive of the question, were the circumstances as they appeared to him—for you require under these circumstances to put yourself in his place, and to ascertain not merely what were the facts but how did they appear to him—what would he as a reasonable man, taking all that he heard and believed, and the information brought to him, the circumstances under which he was placed, and all the rest of it, what would he think, supposing he brought, as I think he was bound to bring, ordinary firmness and moderation in the discharge of his duty,—remembering that his duty was not only to protect the colony, which it clearly was, but also to regard the rights of individuals, and not to oppress and injure them; would a person bringing that proper degree of calmness into operation perceive that what he did was in excess?—that would be a question entirely of fact, and one for you to consider. Upon the evidence, was there excess on his part to the extent that would make him criminally responsible? The degree of criminal excess, as I said a little while ago about criminal negligence, is hard to define, and must be, as a question of common sense, decided by the jury, taking all the facts, together.

Now, gentlemen, I shall afterwards proceed to state to you the nature of the charge that is going to be brought before you, for I have been furnished with a copy of the bill which they intend to lay before you, and then I will call your attention to the evidence which is going to be brought before you (for owing to this case having been, as it ought to have been, before a magistrate, and depositions being taken, I am aware what the evidence is that is going to be before you), and in doing that, I will call your attention to what I have just now said with regard to the law, and give you some remarks to enable you to apply it to the evidence before you. But before we come to that, it is necessary to inquire into a matter which you will perceive is of the very last importance, viz.—What were the limits of Mr. Eyre's powers as a Governor of Jamaica, under the circumstances of the case; what could he do; what power had the law given him to do, so that, when circumstances required the exercise of those powers, he would be bound to exercise them, and in an extreme case, would be punishable for not exercising them? If he has gone quite beyond those, the case would be simple and straightforward, and you would have nothing to do but, if you believe the facts to be so, to find the bill. Then comes the question—What were the powers of the Governor of Jamaica at that time? That must depend upon the law that was in force in Jamaica, and upon that, which is a very important matter, I will explain to you it would hardly be a question for you, it would be more a question of law for me—at least practically. Generally it is said, where there is a foreign law, (and a colonial law is the same,) that is a question of fact to be proved, and the judge is not expected to know it; therefore it might be said to be a question of fact for you, as the jury, to say what the law of Jamaica was; but practically you may be saved the trouble of inquiring into that: it is a matter depending upon principles of law, and upon statutes, and I do not think you would wish at all to take the responsibility upon yourselves of deciding that. I must not shrink from it, and I think it will be very much the same thing whether I say this is technically a question for you, but that I think the law of Jamaica is so and so, and advise you to find that, or direct you upon it as a matter of law; in either case I am responsible for what I tell you, and I do not think you would differ from me, or wish to do so, on such a point.

The first thing I must tell you is generally about the law of colonies. I believe there is no doubt about it, although I perceive, from the argument of Counsel, some points have been thrown out on different sides as to which

I do not agree. I believe, as a point of law, there is no doubt about this, that when a colony is settled, the settlers going out, and settling on waste lands, carry with them the law of England, such as it was at the time they settled in the colony. The difficulties of applying it, at the first starting, are of course considerable. When people go out and make a settlement in a waste colony, for a little time they have no magistrates, courts of justice, or the rest. There is a difficulty, at first starting, we need not concern ourselves with, but they carry out with them the law of England as it was at that time, with its full privileges; they lose no privileges by going to a foreign country, but they remain Englishmen with all their full privileges. Where a colony is acquired by conquest, and where it had a foreign law, in force, as in the case of Trinidad, and other places which belonged to the Spaniards, and where the Spanish law was established; or in the case of the Mauritius, where the French law was established; or the case of Grenada and Demerara, where the Dutch law was in force, I believe there is no doubt that the Crown has an option, and one of its powers in such a case is either to leave the law which was in force in the country at that time still in force, which has been done in most cases— the Spanish where the Spanish law was established, and the Dutch where the Dutch law was established, and so on—or the Crown has the power, upon a conquest, to change that law, to abolish it, and to substitute the English law. Whether it could go further, and substitute any other law or not, is immaterial for us to consider at present, and I express no opinion upon it. But in the case of a conquered country, that the Crown may leave it, or change it to English law is quite certain.

Now, in Jamaica, it appears that the historical difficulty has been considerable to say which of those two it is; one or the other it certainly is. You are aware that in the time of Oliver Cromwell the Spaniards had a settlement in

Jamaica, but Oliver Cromwell took possession of the island, and, in the reign of Charles the Second, we find the English were settling, and Charles the Second made a proclamation offering land to those that settled there, and the English law was then in force. People have differed as to the matter; great Judges have considered it. Lord Mansfield came to the conclusion that the Spaniards had been totally driven out, and consequently it was a settled colony, because the island was then vacant, and the English colonists went out and settled there. Then Lord Wensleydale, I see, in another case, takes the other view of the matter, and says he thinks it was a Spanish colony, and that what we must take as the origin of it was that the prerogative of the Crown was exercised to change the Spanish law to English. It would not make any practical difference which is right. At any rate we have this, that in the reign of Charles the Second the law of England as it was in the reign of Charles the Second was in force in the colony.

Then comes a further question of very great importance to be considered here. I think there is no doubt about it myself, but I must explain it to you: the colony thus established, if the law remained, unless the Imperial Legislature made alterations in it, the law would always remain the same, stereotyped, which would be extremely inconvenient; and it certainly is, I think, established that the Crown has by its prerogative in such a case a right to grant to the colony a Legislative Assembly to make laws within the local jurisdiction of the colony itself, and to alter the English law, in the same way as our Parliament here could alter it; to make colonial Acts, which bind within the limits of the colony to the same extent as English statutes would bind here. Upon that there has been a doubt raised. I was rather surprised to see it. It is the argument of Counsel that the Colonial

Legislature has no power to alter the law at all; that it could not make an Act of a Colonial Legislature which would interfere with or alter the privileges of Englishmen, or extend the law beyond what it had been before. As I have said, I do not entertain any doubt upon this, and I will cite the language of a very learned judge delivering judgments in two cases before the Judicial Committee of the Privy Council, which is the supreme appeal court for every matter from the colonies, and I think that will leave no doubt at all that that is quite a mistake. The first of those cases is one called Beaumont *v.* Barrett, 1st Moore's Privy Council Cases. It came before the Privy Council in this manner. Mr. Beaumont had been in Jamaica, and had been committed by the Legislative Assembly—a body equivalent to the House of Commons— for a contempt of them, and they exercising the power which it is uncontested the House of Commons have, voted it a contempt, and committed Mr. Beaumont to custody for having done so. Mr. Beaumont brought his action against them, treating his imprisonment as illegal, and saying they were exercising a power which they had not got, and the Courts in Jamaica decided they had the power. The question came before the Judicial Committee of the Privy Council, on appeal, to determine whether the Legislative Assembly of Jamaica was like the House of Commons to that extent. In considering that, the learned Judge who delivered the opinion of the Judicial Committee, Mr. Baron Parke—afterwards Lord Wensleydale— after stating that the grant of the Crown created a Legislative Assembly, says, " And it gives that body the power, subordinate, no doubt, to that of the Parliament of Great Britain, and subject to its control, if it chooses to exercise it, to make laws which will bind all the inhabitants of Jamaica and its dependencies. This Assembly is not like a corporation which has a power to make by-laws for the carrying into effect the purpose for which it was established, but it is the supreme Legislative Assembly of the island, authorised to make laws for it with the sanction of the Sovereign." You will observe that Mr. Baron Parke, a most learned and cautious judge, puts in the words "subordinate, no doubt, to the Parliament of Great Britain, and subject to its control, if they choose to exercise it." There is no doubt that is the law as it stands in England; the Imperial Legislature is supreme, and when the Imperial Legislature chooses to make an enactment contrary to that of the Legislative Assembly, we must, in England, say that the Imperial Legislature prevails. In the Navigation Laws there are express enactments that the colonists should not make laws to allow foreigners to trade with the colonies, and there they exercise the control which they had a right to exercise; and where that is done, no doubt the Colonial Legislature cannot make a law which would be binding in contradiction to the Imperial Legislature. Again, although the general rule is that the Legislative Assembly has the sole right of imposing taxes in the colony, when the Imperial Legislature chooses to impose taxes, according to the rule of English law they have a right to do it. You are well aware that in the United States, which were colonies having Legislative Assemblies, just as the Legislative Assembly of Jamaica in this case, the Imperial Legislature did choose to exercise the power of imposing taxes; the colonists resisted that, and we all know that it ended in their becoming the United States. As to their right morally, we have nothing to do with that. As a question of English law, there is no doubt we must say, as Baron Parke in that case said, that all legislatures of the colonies were subject to the control of the Imperial Legislature; therefore, whatever may be the moral rights, upon the legal question, in our courts, the colonies were wrong, and the Imperial Parliament was right. But that does not at all extend to show that the Colonial Legislature cannot

F

make Acts of Parliament which would interfere with the English statutes and laws as they existed at the time they were colonised; to say that would be, in effect, to say that they cannot change the law at all.

I have cited a case, in which the Judicial Committee of the Privy Council came to the conclusion, that the Legislative Assembly was so like the House of Commons, that it had the power of committing for contempt. Afterwards, at a subsequent time, very nearly the same point came before the Judicial Committee of the Privy Council, which arose in the case of Newfoundland. That had been a settled colony, but so recently as the year 1836, the Crown granted a Legislative Assembly for the first time; that grant was not by Act of Parliament at all, but was exercised by the prerogative of the Crown. That newly constituted assembly exercised the same power as the Legislative Assembly in Jamaica had done, and committed for contempt. The question was brought before the Judicial Committee of the Privy Council, and they had had to reconsider the question that arose in the case of Beaumont and Barrett. The case I am now referring to is the case of Keeley *v.* Carson, page 65 of the 4th vol. of Moore's Privy Council Cases, and there the question was argued and considered very carefully before the Court, which I think you will admit carried with it, as then composed, independently of its being the supreme court for deciding all colonial matters, the highest authority. I will give you the names of the judges who considered the case, Lord Lyndhurst the then Lord Chancellor, Lord Brougham, Lord Denman, Lord Abinger, Lord Cottenham, Lord Campbell, Sir Launcelot Shadwell, the Vice-Chancellor of England, the Chief Justice of the Common Pleas, Sir Nicholas Tindal, Mr. Baron Parke, Mr. Justice Erskine, and Dr. Lushington, a Court than which I think, when you hear all their names, and consider who they were, you will say none could be more competent to decide

the matter that they had to consider, which was the
power of the Legislative Council in Newfoundland. And
they, including Mr. Baron Parke, came to a different conclusion to that which the Committee had come to in the
case of Beaumont *v.* Barrett; that shows how carefully
they considered the matter. Mr. Baron Parke, who had
changed his opinion and joined the majority, then delivered
judgment, and what he said was this—" Newfoundland is
a settled, not a conquered colony, and to such a colony
there is no doubt that the settlers from the mother country
carried with them such a portion of its common and
statute law as was applicable to their new situation, and
also the rights and immunities of British subjects. Their
descendants have, on the other hand, the same laws and the
same rights, unless they have been altered by Parliament.
And upon the other hand, the Crown possesses the same
prerogatives and the same powers of government that it
does over its other subjects. Nor has it been disputed that
the Sovereign had the right of erecting a local Legislative
Assembly, with authority subordinate, indeed, to Parliament, but supreme within the limits of the colony, for the
government of its inhabitants." Then he states the question upon which his former opinion was changed, that although the Legislative Assembly was supreme, yet the power
of committing for contempt, exercised by the House of
Commons, was not incident to that, consequently his former
decision was a mistake ; but you will observe that he puts
it as perfectly clear, that they have the supreme legislative power within the limits of the colony, subject to the
control of Parliament. It may be, for anything I know to
the contrary, that this may not be law, and that in a civil
case persons may go into the House of Lords, or to the Judicial Committee of the Privy Council, and succeed in showing
that all this was a mistake, and that a Colonial Act of the
Legislature is not supreme, and that a person who acts in
obedience to the colonial law, is liable if the Colonial
law is shown to be unconstitutional, and *ultra vires* in the

F 2

sense in which they say an Act proclaiming martial law in Jamaica is. It may be, though it is contrary to my opinion, that they would succeed in doing that. But here we are dealing with a question of criminal law, and I think I should be wrong if I left you in any doubt about it. It is impossible to say we ever could punish a person, in Jamaica or in any colony, where there is a Legislative Assembly, for acting *bona fide* and honestly under a Legislative Act of the Colonial Parliament. It would be monstrous that he should be bound to take upon himself to say whether such an Act of Parliament is binding or not, and to say "I will not obey it because I think it is unconstitutional." There is such a power given to the supreme courts in America, but there is no such power in the English courts. A party could not be bound to disobey the law at any risk, and it would, I think, be impossible, if he obeyed it, for any one to support the proposition that he could be criminally punished for that.

Therefore, I think we must start here by saying that Mr. Eyre, as Governor of Jamaica at that time, had not only those powers which, in the reign of Charles II., at the time the colony was established, the Crown had by its prerogative, and which he as Governor would have as representing the Crown; but he has also those powers which were given him by the Acts of the Colonial Legislature, and this is a point of immense importance in the present case; and I think I should be wrong if I left you in any doubt whatever that that is the rule of law upon which you are to go. Then come the two questions, What was the prerogative of the Crown in respect of this matter at the time of Charles II., *i.e.*, to proclaim martial law? and to what extent have the statutes of the Colonial Legislature given Mr. Eyre more or greater power than that? When we have ascertained that as a matter of law, then the question will become ripe for you to determine, as a matter of fact, whether he has transgressed his powers or not.

Now, as to that question, What was the construction of Acts of the Colonial Legislature? very much depends upon seeing what the law was in the time of Charles II., and what it was supposed to be. In construing an Act of Legislature, as common sense will tell you at once, you look to what was the law, or what was supposed to be the law before,—what was it the Legislature meant to do? what was their object? what was the defect of the Common Law which they were seeking to remedy and change?—and you then consider the words, and see what they really have done for the purpose of carrying that out. Therefore it is necessary, to that extent, to inquire what the prerogative was at the time of Charles II., for the purpose of ascertaining the meaning of the Colonial Act. Further than that it is not necessary to decide, except this, whether or not the prerogative as it existed then would justify such extensive measures as have been taken I do not think it would; but further than that it is not necessary to go; and certainly I am unwilling to give any opinion upon anything that is unnecessary, because there is a great deal of doubt as to what the law is, and therefore I do not feel it proper for me to do anything that is unnecessary which could be cited hereafter as a decision. I wish to avoid stating more than is necessary for the present case; but, to a certain extent, it is necessary to consider that question.

Now you, all of you, know, that by the laws of this country, beginning at Magna Charta and getting more and more established, down to the time of the Revolution, when it was finally and completely established, the general rule was that a subject was not to be tried or punished, except by due course of law; all crimes are to be determined by juries, subject to the guidance of the judge: that is the general rule, and is established law. But from the earliest times there was this also which was the law, and is the law still, that when there was a foreign invasion or an insurrection, it was the duty of every good subject, in obedience to the officers and magistrates, to resist the rebels, and for the purpose of resisting them the executive officer could call them out, and, in point of fact, raise an army in order to fight them. In modern times that has become of little consequence, because we have, under the Mutiny Acts, and the Militia Statute and others, an armed force which can be raised and subject to the control of the law according to the statutes; and it is of very little practical consequence now, but in old times, in the age of Magna Charta, which was finally confirmed by Henry III.; during all the barons' wars, and afterwards, when there was no regular army, when there was an insurrection, to meet it, there were persons intrusted with Commissions of Array from the Crown to raise an army to fight the insurgents. As to that, everybody must feel at once that an armed force that was only to be punished by juries would be an intolerable nuisance, and could not be endured at all. Consequently, the prerogative was claimed by the Crown, that the Crown by its prerogative might direct that its armed force should be kept in order by summary process; not by a despotism which would authorise its officers to kill anyone they pleased, but summary process, not waiting for the ordinary process of the common law, to keep the soldiers in order; and in that sense there was a martial law, terribly liable to be' abused no doubt, but which Lord Hale has said, in a passage frequently quoted, was tolerated and excused because it was really the absence of all law; and that prerogative existed certainly, I think, in time of war, and the Crown had that prerogative over that armed force which it had gathered together for the purpose of fighting the enemy, whether a foreign enemy or an army in insurrection; and to that extent I think the Crown had the power to exercise martial law in time of war, and in time of war only. Further than that, there was what comes on very debateable ground indeed: in such a case as that of insurrection prevailing so far that the courts of law cannot sit, there must really be anarchy unless there is some power to keep the people in order. Supposing an invading army, for instance, took possession of Dover, and an English army lay opposite to them, you could have no Court of Quarter Sessions sitting in Kent and no Assizes there; and really unless you were to have some power to keep order there would be total anarchy. Upon that principle, the Crown claimed the prerogative in those early times (most fortunately now we have not the occasion to consider this question at all) to exercise summary proceedings by martial law, as they called it, in time of war, when this disturbance was going on, over others than the army. And further than that, the Crown made this further claim against the insurgents, that whilst it existed, pending the insurrection, and for a short time afterwards, the Crown had, and *de facto* exercised, the power to proclaim martial law, in the sense of using summary proceedings, to punish the insurgents, and to check and stop the spread of the rebellion by summary proceedings against the insurgents, so as, to adopt a modern phrase, " to stamp out the rebellion." Now no doubt the extent to which the Crown had power to do that has never been yet decided. Our law has been declared from time to time, and has always been a practical science; that is, the judges have decided so much as was necessary for the particular case, and that has become part of the law. But it never has come to be decided what this precise power is. The Crown did in fact exercise that power to some extent, at least in time of war, and in a way which was productive frequently of immense oppression. The last time, as far as I am aware, of its being exercised to any considerable extent was in the reign of Queen Elizabeth, at the time of the rising in the North under the Earls of Westmoreland and Northumberland, when they raised the northern counties; and after they were defeated, after the army had broken them down, there was a great deal of the process of summary execution done. You will see an account of it in the last volume of Froude's History, and a great deal of tyranny was, no doubt exercised; in point of fact, a great deal of summary trial and execution took place in a way which, according to our modern view, was most tyrannical and oppressive, and which would not be sanctioned now. After that, when things had become rather more orderly, the power fell into the hands of James I. Queen Elizabeth was a person of great sense and had very wise statesmen and councillors; she did strong acts and used mild words, while James I. seemed rather to do the reverse. He, it has been said, used stronger expressions but did weaker acts: and so he at once aroused and encouraged opposition. In the beginning of the reign of Charles I. this had been done; the Crown, in time of peace, chose to raise an armed force, a small standing army, and with a view to have that standing army kept in order the king issued commissions which distinctly and in terms claimed those powers. I will read the terms of the commission:—" To proceed with power and authority against such soldiers and all other dissolute persons, not only for mutiny but for any felony or offence, and, by such summary order as is agreeable to martial law, and as is used in armies in time of war, to cause them to be executed according to martial law." That is the commission which they issued in time of peace, the right to do which was opposed in the Parliament which met in the reign of Charles I. and passed the Petition of Right, which you have all heard of, distinctly denouncing that, and reciting that this had been done, and after reciting that all this was illegal, they " do humbly pray that the aforesaid commissions for proceeding by martial law may be revoked and annulled: and that hereafter no commissions of like nature may issue forth to be executed as aforesaid, lest by colour of them any subjects be destroyed or put to death contrary to law." You will observe that the Petition in terms says that " no commissions of the like nature shall issue ;" that is, commissions to proceed, in time of peace, "in such summary course as is used in time of war in armies." The Legislature, therefore, did not in terms declare that in time of war they shall not have the power, but it does not by any means follow that they sanctioned and recognised that doing so in time of war was legal. I do not think that would be a reasonable inference at all. The great statesmen as well as great lawyers at that time in Parliament were sensible enough to be aware that in fighting with the Crown at such a time they should take care that they were distinctly in the right ; that there should be no doubt about the point on which they took their stand. They did not, therefore, say that Queen Elizabeth did such things at the time of the rising in the North as were illegal ; it would have been very foolish of them to do that, because by attacking the Crown on such a point, they would have given the Crown a debateable ground which would have been of immense advantage to it. It may be very much doubted, too, whether the Puritans, who were the great party who struggled against Charles, would have altogether sympathised with the implied attack on the Protestant Queen Elizabeth if it had been made, for the mode in which she put down the two Popish earls for the rising in the North; and they, therefore, as wise statesmen, did not take that point. I think, therefore, it would be an exceedingly wrong presumption to say that the Petition of Right, by not condemning martial law in time of war, sanctioned it, still it did not in terms condemn it.

There never has been since that time any case in which it has become necessary to consider judicially what were the limits of the powers of the prerogative in time of war. This much, I think, I may safely say, that in time of peace the Crown has no such power. Lord Hale, in a work, I believe, never published by him, but found amongst his papers after his death, " The Analysis of the Law," says the Crown, by its prerogative, has the power of punishing rebels " during the rebellion, but not after." I am quoting from memory, but I think that is it, and then, in a passage which you find often quoted in his " History of the Common Law," he in effect says, " Martial law is that which is the absence of all law, tolerated for necessity, where necessity requires it, but confined strictly to the army on the part of the Crown and those who are against them." That is the substance, but it would seem he had changed his mind somewhat during that time, and he has put down very different views. Then, when he came to publish his great work, " The Pleas of the Crown," his deliberately and carefully prepared work, he was very cautious indeed. In a passage which has been cited, 1st vol., p. 347, he puts it, after citing the case of the Earl of Lancaster, " From this record it will appear that in time of peace the Crown cannot enforce martial law ;" and further, that " *regularly*, when the King's Courts are open it is a time of peace in judgment of laws." He is very cautious, you will observe, and puts it there in this way, and that is certainly the opinion I have come to myself, that it has not been quite settled what is the Crown's prerogative in such cases, and what not. But I think this much is settled, that it is by no means that unbounded, wild, and tyrannical prerogative which some persons have lately been saying that it is. It must, if it exist at all, be strictly limited to necessity, and I think you cannot doubt that Mr. Eyre, in keeping up martial law, for thirty days; after all armed resistance had been put down in a day or two,—so that there was really a period of three or four weeks after all armed resistance had ceased, when it would have been quite practicable to try any one by the ordinary tribunals; there can be no reasonable doubt that he did exceed much that would be authorised on the most extended view of the prerogative. To that extent, I think, I am bound to go ; more than that, I think is unnecessary in this case. Beyond what I have said I will leave the case to be decided when it arises, without being biased by any weight of authority that might be attached to what I say, but to that extent, I think, I am bound to express an opinion. Therefore, if it stood solely and entirely on the question of what was the power which Mr. Eyre had in exercising the common law prerogative of the Crown, I think I should be obliged to say to you that, though there might be very good reasons for an Act of Indemnity or for a pardon, that you must find this bill. But then the law by no means remains in that state in Jamaica; it has been completely altered by the Jamaica Statutes, as I construe them, and very greatly extended power is given to the Governor of Jamaica more than ever was possessed by the Crown in this country, or by the officers of the Crown in this country, except in Ireland, when, by the Act of Parliament, martial law was enforced ; and what the Legislature sanctioned was law for the time being, just as what the Legislature of Jamaica sanctioned was law in Jamaica.

Now, the first Act that passed, which is one of the first of the Colonial Legislature, was the 33rd Charles II. (if not in the very first session of the Legislature, the second), when the Legislature were making an enactment for the purpose of establishing a militia. You must remember that the colonists carried out with them, or they had given them by the Crown, superseding the Spanish law (it matters not which), the law as it was in the time of Charles II., and the Petition of Right was part of that law, and consequently neither the Crown nor the Governor had got the least right, in time of peace, of regulating an army by martial law, still less of declaring martial law in the sense of superseding the common law and deciding that the people should be tried by summary process, although the courts of law were open. The Jamaica Legislature, having that before them, knew what the law was, and what had been claimed by the Crown, and what had been refused by the English Parliament. I suppose the Governor was probably inclined to the high prerogative view, but the colonists would have every wish to protect themselves from oppression, but they knew perfectly well that they were a slave colony, and that insurrections were very likely to occur, and that they were in a freshly conquered colony, surrounded by Spanish colonists, and likely to be invaded from abroad; and that being so, the Legislature passed the Militia Act, and in many clauses they provided that everybody was to be a member of that militia. And, then, I wish to call attention to this—the militia were to be called out in time of peace, and to be subject to martial law, and punished by martial law, and punished by the officers holding courts-martial; but, there is this limitation, that the power of court-martial to punish them shall not extend to life or limb. There are some curious quaint provisions in the Act as to the sort of punishment. One seems to be to tie them hand and foot to a wooden horse and tie them up, which, I should have thought, in such a climate as that of Jamaica, would probably endanger life or limb. Still the important point upon that is, that during the time there was no war, they did grant a power which the Petition of Right said the Crown had not—power to organise the militia and have it under the control of martial law.

Then comes the important section in this Act. It has been since repealed, but it was an enactment which I consider to be the one which we have now most to consider. "Be it enacted that upon every apprehension and appearance of any public danger or invasion, the Commander-in-chief shall forthwith call a Council of War, and with their advice and consent cause and command the Articles of War to be proclaimed;" and "that then it shall and may be lawful for the said Commander-in-chief to command the persons of any of His Majesty's liege subjects, as also their negroes, horses, and cattle, for all such services as may be for the public defence, and to pull down houses, cut down timber, and command ships and boats, and generally to act and do with full power and authority all such things as he and the said Council of War may think necessary and expedient for His Majesty's service and the defence of this island." " Provided always, that as soon as the common law is revived and is in force, the said negroes, horses and cattle, and so forth, shall be immediately discharged; and to the end that it may be certainly known when the martial law ceases and the common law taketh place, be it declared that when the colours shall no longer be flying, the martial law shall cease and the common law revive."

Now, gentlemen, what does that mean? I must acknowledge that when I look at that Act, and consider the words, and the object the Jamaica Legislature had in view at that time, I can have no doubt. It has, I know, been argued and urged that the only intention was that they might have martial law in the same sense as in the Mutiny Act, that they might call out the militia and put martial law in force to control the militia; but that had been already provided for by the former section; and the Act provides that when the occasion ceases, " martial law shall cease and the common law revive." Looking at those words, I can put but one sense or meaning on them. I do not know how it may strike others. I think that the Legislature of Jamaica meant to enact that the Commander-in-chief at the time should have very extensive power, upon "the apprehension or appearance of any public danger or invasion," that then he should have power, with the advice of a Council of War, to do that which the Petition of Right had declared the Crown could not do in time of peace, and which it is doubtful whether the Crown could ever legally do in time of war; I mean, to supersede the common law altogether, and to punish all manner of offences that were then done; by summary process, not of course to give arbitrary power like that which it is said an Oriental sovereign has, to kill men with cause or without cause, but to enable the authorities to supersede the ordinary process of law, the ordinary common law, and to try all manner of things by this summary process, in order that offenders might be summarily tried and punished; the great object being to stop the invasion or insurrection. This very arbitrary and great power was, I think, granted to the Commander-in-chief by that statute.

After that statute a great many different statutes were passed relating to the regulation of the militia, and all were in force until as late as the time of the passing of the 9th Victoria, after Jamaica had ceased to be a slave colony altogether, in 1845; as late as that the 9th of Victoria was passed. It was an Act enumerating and repealing in the first section all the former militia Acts, including that of Charles the Second, and substituting provisions with which I do not think I need trouble you much, until I am at that part which is substituted for that provision of the 33rd Charles the Second, which I have read to you. It says:—"And whereas it is fit to ascertain who shall compose the Council of War, be it further enacted that all Councils of War shall consist of the Governor and Commander-in-chief for the time being, the Admiral and Commander-in-chief of His Majesty's ships on the station for the time being, the several Members of the Privy Council, the Speaker and Members of the Assembly, general officers of militia." Not less than twenty-one to form a Council of War. Then it provides by another section that, in case that Assembly shall be dissolved, the members of the late Assembly shall get together. So thus they declare what the Council of War shall be; that it shall include all the notables of the island, the people who hold high offices, and that body the Legislature considers it to be the Council of War, to whom, and under whose sanction, you will find in the next section they entrust very extensive powers. And then comes this:— "And whereas the appearance of public danger by invasion or otherwise may sometimes make the imposition of martial law necessary, yet, as from experience of the mischief and calamities attending it, it must ever be considered as among the greatest evils, be it enacted that it shall not in future be declared or imposed but by the opinion and advice of a Council of War consisting as aforesaid." Then comes a provision that the martial law may be proclaimed in parts of the island without being proclaimed in all. That was the statute which was in force at the time Mr. Eyre succeeded to the Governorship.

Now comes the question—What power was it that that gave him? I have read the words, and you have heard them. I have pointed out to you that I think there can be no doubt that the original Act of Charles the Second was intended to give power to exercise martial law in the fullest sense; when it ceases, "the common law revives," is the very phrase that is used. I do not find in any of the numerous intermediate Militia Acts that there has been any definition given of what the martial law was intended to be. I do find as a fact that there were numerous insurrections of slaves in the island, when vast numbers of things were done which perhaps could not be justified even under martial law, but which certainly could not be unless martial law existed to that extent. I am aware that it has been said these acts might be justified under various Acts of the local Legislature applying to slaves, according to which, if I understand the reasoning rightly, the slaves were not, in fact, to be treated as human beings, but were as animals, except so far as partial privileges had been given them; and that when there was an insurrection those privileges were gone, and the slave might be killed on the same principle as you would kill a wolf or a dog. I do not pretend to know the Acts of the Jamaica Legislature. I have not looked into them, but I know that in slave states there is very likely to have been very fearful legislation; but I must venture to say, and I think you will agree, that no such ground of justification was ever put forward in this country. It is a dangerous thing to assert the negative, but I think you will agree with me in this case, and I will tell you why. I am old. enough to remember the last insurrection in Jamaica, which I think was in 1830: there was a good deal done at that time very difficult to defend. The Anti-Slave Society had just come to the point of succeeding in abolishing Slavery altogether, and their leaders in Parliament, Lord Brougham, then Mr. Brougham, Dr. Lushington, and Sir Fowell Buxton were all in their full vigour; and we know very well, if any defence of the proceedings in Jamaica had been put forward on the ground which has now been suggested to be the ground—that the slave was a beast; that he had no privilege except that given him by special law, and that he had lost that ;—I think I know in what way those gentlemen would have met it. I think I may venture to say Lord Brougham (putting aside all the others) would have said something about it we should all have heard of and should not have forgotten. I think, therefore, I am justified in saying that that ground was never put forward at all, and I cannot doubt, when you read the words of the 9th Victoria, which says, from "experience of the mischiefs of martial law, it must ever be considered as amongst the greatest evils ;"—I do not think you can doubt at all what the Legislature of Jamaica were then meaning and thinking was, "that martial law in such a country as ours may be necessary in the sense of superseding the common law, but we think it would be necessary to put two checks upon it, that it shall never be proclaimed or put in force without the full consent of the Council of War, consisting of all the notables of the island; and secondly, it shall *ipso facto* cease at the end of thirty days, unless the same Council of War shall see fit to prolong it."

Now, I think, I have very nearly done with all that may be considered as direction on a point of law to you. I shall have to give you assistance in enabling you to perform your part; I have very nearly finished as to the law. I think, under those Acts of the Colonial Legislature, Governor Eyre, in case of invasion or apprehended invasion, might, with the consent of the Council of War, have the power to proclaim martial law in any district of the country, in the sense that it superseded the common law for the time being, and enabled all matters to be tried by summary procedure (that is the phrase with regard to what was forbidden in the Petition of Right), "by such summary procedure as is used in time of war," not with an arbitrary discretion, but without applying mere technical rules: so as to do the substance of justice in a summary way. Such power he might have on proper occasions, and exercise it. Consequently, if there was a state of things such as, to borrow the language of the King *v.* Pinney, that a firm, reasonable man would have felt that he ought to have used this power, and he did not do so, he would have been punishable for it. I think, as I said before, that a man is bound to exercise reasonable firmness and moderation in determining whether he should do it or not.* If a man of reasonable firmness, self-control, and moderation would not have done it, then, I have no doubt, he would have been punishable for the want of that firmness and moderation; but there would come to be a question upon that for you. Put yourself in his place, knowing what he did know, and see whether there was a criminal neglect to bring that reasonable firmness, self-control, and moderation to bear on the question. Then, secondly, when martial law had been proclaimed, Mr. Eyre might have stopped it before thirty days, but he allowed it to continue, and there, again, there arises a question. First, the

---

* But it is to be observed that in Rex *v.* Pinney that was laid down of the conduct of the magistrate in the *earlier* stages of the disturbances, when they were mere ordinary *riots*, easily repressible by ordinary means, and by means distinctly provided by ordinary municipal law. And it was laid down also that a magistrate is only bound to have ordinary firmness, i.e., *sufficient for an ordinary emergency*. And it was further laid down that he is not expected to deal with riots going on in various places. See the case cited in the *Review of the Authorities*.

G

question is—Whether he could properly proclaim martial law? and I think there was not much doubt, under the circumstances, that he would have been culpable if he had not. But now comes the second question—Is he punishable for not having stopped it sooner? and that depends very much upon the state of things as they appeared before him and as they will appear to you. What did he do? As to that, I think, when we look at the Act of the Colonial Legislature, what they meant was that summary jurisdiction might continue so long as was necessary to prevent the insurrection going on. He was to try men fairly and properly, so far as could be done, but he might try them summarily, and, when it was necessary, where there was danger that, if he did not exercise such summary jurisdiction, insurrection might spread and the country be destroyed, then, I think, the Colonial Legislature gave the Governor power that he might do it. Then comes the question, and an important one—Had he such reasonable grounds as to lead him to think it right to continue it; or did he continue it, in fact, to such an excess and degree, and so much more than was necessary, and so far beyond it, that you would say a man exercising reasonable moderation and firmness which he ought to bring to that purpose, would have known that he should not do it, and must be blamed because he did do it?

This raises a question of fact, upon that part of the case, which must be for you.

There is a third and a great question which I have more doubt about, and that arises from this—when the martial law had been proclaimed in this particular district, Mr. Eyre caused, I think, four different persons, I think not more, to be seized in parts of the island, where martial law was not in force, and to be brought into the district where martial law was in force, in order that they might be tried there, for the offences which they were said to have committed. One of them, as you know, Gordon, was tried, convicted, and executed. The other three were not tried, they were sent for the purpose of trial, and were detained there until martial law had expired, and were ultimately tried by the common law. I think there were four besides Gordon— three were acquitted, and one convicted, but that was only done afterwards; during martial law they were sent for the purpose of trial, and detained. Then comes the question, looking at these colonial Acts, and seeing that the men were in a district where martial law was not proclaimed, but where the Courts of Justice were open, and where they might have been perfectly well tried by the ordinary tribunals, only that there would have been some delay, could it have been a justifiable thing, under those Acts, for the Governor to remove them from the place where they might have been tried by the common law, into a place where martial law had superseded the common law, for the purpose of trying them by martial law,—could that be justified at all? If I thought it never could be right I should tell you at once that you must find a bill on that; was it an act quite beyond his powers, or was it one which might, under proper facts, be justified under the terms of the Acts of the Colonial Legislature? I have considered that carefully myself, with the best lights I could get upon the matter, and I have come to the conclusion that, looking at what martial law was, the bringing of a person into the proclaimed district to be tried, might in a proper case be justified. As a general rule of law all crime is local, and must be tried where it is committed. Exceptions are made in numerous statutes—as for instance, in this very case, we are now trying in the county of Middlesex, matters which occurred in Jamaica; but as a general rule, if a person is arrested in any part of the country for a crime alleged to have been committed in another place, he is regularly and generally sent to that place for the purpose of being tried there. When that place is under martial law, and the common law has been superseded, it becomes a question that should be very carefully and cautiously examined. One great reason for martial law no doubt, and for summary jurisdiction instead of the

G 2

common law, is the impracticability of having a tribunal regularly constituted when the rebellion is going on. You cannot have quarter sessions and assizes, they cannot even sit. There is an impracticability about it. That is one of the great reasons which would justify, on the ground of necessity, having summary process applied.* That would not at all apply to cases of arrest of parties away from where war was going on, where there was no insurrection, although there might be apprehension that one was impending, and where therefore they might easily be apprehended and detained in custody and tried by the ordinary process; and in fact these persons were detained and put on board a ship of war and carried to Morant Bay. There cannot be the smallest doubt that where they were on board the Wolverine, in the custody of Her Majesty's navy and marines, they could have been detained. As far as that goes, there is not the smallest doubt that even if the whole island was in an insurrection, all the negroes of Jamaica could not have taken them out of the frigate. There was not the slightest difficulty in detaining them for any time that was necessary for their trial; but beyond that, what I think the Legislature of Jamaica intended was that, there should be a power of summary trial for the purpose of bringing persons to their trial speedily, so as to have the effect of stopping the insurrection—to use the phrase I did before—to have a summary trial, of course observing all the substantials of justice; but yet to try the man speedily for the purpose of stamping out the insurrection by means of this summary process. I think, therefore, when there was such a case as that of removing Mr. Gordon, which is the more important one to consider, what you have to do is to put yourselves in Mr. Eyre's position, to see what was the motive for this, what were the circumstances and the facts.

---

* Only, it is to be observed, *one* of the reasons. The learned judge, with his accustomed accuracy abstains carefully from implying that this is the only one. There may be other reasons than the absolute impracticability of trials by ordinary process. There may be an urgent necessity for a more speedy process.

I think when you look at the evidence you will not doubt Mr. Gordon had been—I hardly know what word to use—perhaps a pestilent firebrand, and using very violent language indeed, and had been in close communication with these persons who actually murdered the Custos, and the other persons, I do not think you will doubt that; but I do not think there is any evidence that leads to the conclusion that he was more than that. I think he was a violent, pestilent agitator, that he used very improper and very seditious language, which caused this insurrection; but I do not think upon the evidence that he was a party to any organized conspiracy, to cause an insurrection throughout the island. Such an insurrection might be very likely to break out if not checked, but I think, if you look at the evidence, it would not justify the conclusion that he was a party to it. I cannot doubt, however, on looking at the evidence, that there was a general belief in the island that he was so; and certainly many of those around Mr. Eyre believed that he was so, and Mr. Eyre himself probably did believe it, and thought he was really guilty. Upon that the test comes to this, if you think Mr. Eyre thought "Gordon is a fiery, pestilent, and seditious person, and did a great deal of mischief, and if I keep him here and try him by the common law, and ordinary tribunals, the technicalities of the law, and one thing or another, will cause him to be acquitted, and that will be a bad thing, and therefore I will send him to Morant Bay, and cause him to be tried by martial law and get rid of him." If you think that he thought this, I am bound to tell you that would be an act of grave and lawless tyranny and oppression, and a bill should be found at once; but if you come to the conclusion that Mr. Eyre—and here you will have to put yourselves in his position, to see with his eyes, and hear with his ears, you will have, as far as possible, to bring before you that which was before him, and if you come to the conclusion that he thought there was a dangerous insurrection and conspiracy spreading

throughout the island, likely to break into insurrection all
through the island unless it was suppressed, and that it
was really proper for suppressing it, that Mr. Gordon,
whom he believed to be the head, should be summarily
tried—not with a view that he might be convicted, wherein
a regular trial he would not be, but because there was not
time to wait, and it was necessary that the head of the insurrection should be punished promptly with a view to
˙stop it,—if you think that was the state of circumstances,
I am not prepared to say that he might not be fully justified, and, indeed, I think I ought to tell you that he
would be excused in acting under the powers which the
Colonial Legislature had given him, for that purpose, to that
extent. And then comes the question of fact for you to determine, put yourselves, which is not an easy matter to do,
but as far as you can, in the position in which Mr. Eyre was
at the time this matter took place, and say, first, whether
doing that, it was a wrong act? I have told you that
I have come to the conclusion that he was mistaken. You
may come to a different conclusion; it is a matter of fact for
you, and if you come to the conclusion that he was right,
there is an end of it; you would say there was no ground
for charging him. Secondly, if you think he really
honestly and *bonâ fide*, acted not from any motive of getting
rid of Mr. Gordon, but because he thought (though he was
mistaken), that he was guilty, that his summary trial was
necessary, then you would have to say, putting yourselves
as far as you can in his circumstances, making great allowance for the position in which he was, and for his responsibility to the colony—not like us, quietly and coolly, years
afterwards, debating and considering about the matter, but
in a position responsible for the colony, and having everybody round him—for I think that appears to be quite clear
—urging him on, and nobody holding him back; then you
will consider whether, under those circumstances there was
that degree of want of care and reasonable calmness and
moderation which I think a man in his position was bound

to exercise, as would make him criminally responsible. It is a question of more or less. That is a difficult question, and one which I am sorry to leave to you with so little assistance, but I think that is the point for you to consider.

The other three parties were brought into custody and detained, but not actually tried. They were sent for the purposes of trial, but not actually tried. The same observation applies to them, but I need hardly say their cases are far lighter ones. If you come to the conclusion that Mr. Eyre was not guilty of criminal excess in causing Gordon to be actually tried and executed, you will probably come to the conclusion that there was no criminal excess in causing the others to be sent for trial. The same principle prevails, but that would be a much easier case to decide.

That, I think, really concludes all I shall say to you as positive direction on points of law. You must see at once that what I have said involves points of very great importance, not merely for decision in this particular case, but for the guidance of persons in authority, in colonies and elsewhere, and that it is a matter of great importance; I am sorry, from the nature of the case, and the way it is brought before us, that I am obliged to take upon myself singly the responsibility of looking up the case and laying down the law. I need not tell you that I have bestowed anxious consideration on it, and have been reading carefully what has been said by others before. I have taken every possible opportunity of consulting with any of my brother judges as far as I could get their advice and assistance upon it. None of them have had the opportunity to consider it judicially as I have done. Several of them have given me assistance here and there upon different points, and I think I may say that most of those to whom I have spoken are agreed in all I have said. Upon one point I should qualify this. I have laid it down, and you must take it as a rule of law, that even if there was perfect innocence and honesty of intention, yet, if there was a failure of exercising that degree of calmness, moderation, and self-control, which a man might be expected reasonably to have, the Governor would be responsible for that. One learned judge when I consulted him intimated an opinion that he hardly thought it would go so far as that, but that there must be a guilty intention. I have considered the matter since, and, principally upon the authority of the King *v.* Pinney, but also upon general rules of law, I came to the conclusion I have stated to you. I do not know whether that learned judge still would differ from me, for I have not had an opportunity of seeing him since. I finally made up my mind, and I cannot say whether he differs from me or not, but I advise you to follow the rule as I lay it down. If there is any bill found by you, then it will be proper to have this point considered afterwards more deliberately. At present I think you should follow the view that I am telling you, that is, the view of what I think the law should be; and I may state further, as to the judges of my own court, the Lord Chief Justice, my brother Mellor, my brother Lush, and my brother Hannen, with whom I have communication every day, I have had much more frequent opportunity of consulting with them, and finally, yesterday, I stated to them the effect of what I am now stating to you, and they all approved of it, and authorised me to say (of course not relieving me from my responsibility, or absolutely binding them, for of course they have not considered it so thoroughly and so judicially as I have been obliged to do,) still, they authorise me to say they agree in my view of the law, and thought it right.* I mention that because it is very desirable

---

* There was afterwards some appearance of a misunderstanding as to this, but the statement was repeated by the learned Judge; and on a close attention to the language of the Lord Chief Justice in his observations on the point (vide Appendix), it will be seen that it is not, in substance, invalidated, but is substantially supported, and that there was no *dissent* as to any *legal* proposition.

it should not be supposed this is only my own view. It is the view that has been entertained by the best authorities we can get upon the subject.

Now, gentlemen, I have finished all that is positive direction to you, and I will now proceed to do what will be rather assisting you in your task. You will have perceived what is the general outline of your duty. I know what the indictment is that is to be preferred before you, and what the charges are that you will have to consider, and I know also from the depositions what the evidence is that will be brought before you; and I will help you as well as I can by pointing out what the evidence is, and what the charges are, and then make such remarks as occur to me upon the bearing of that evidence on the charges, to assist you, not as directing you at all, but to assist you in the very difficult and troublesome task in which you will be very glad to get assistance, but cannot be directed. You are bound by your oaths to act for yourselves, of course taking the law from me; but when I give you assistance upon facts, you will consider that with respect and attention of course, but you will not consider that as direction. You will act upon your own notion of what the facts are, not upon mine.

Now I come to what the evidence is. First, I will take what evidence has been brought before me. You know that a Royal Commission was sent out to Jamaica to inquire into all these matters, and this Commission had to examine all manner of witnesses, and, generally, to every one who came, they made them aware that they need not answer any questions that might criminate themselves, or state what would be evidence against them at a future time. Amongst others, the Commission had before them Mr. Eyre. Of course he was told this, but he scorned to take advantage of anything of the sort. He thought that he had been right. Of course you will not go upon what he thought, but what really he did. But he thought he was more to be praised and lauded for what he had done than punished, and he answered everything fairly, fully, and frankly, and afterwards at a later day,' he came and said he wished to add some explanations which he thought justified him, and he proceeded to make his own statement upon various matters, but upon which I do not think, when I read the second portion, that he mended the matter beyond what he had already done in his former examination; but there it is. The first piece of evidence that we have is what Mr. Eyre stated, and which will be brought before you. Strictly, the shorthand-writers, the persons present who heard it, should be asked, what did Mr. Eyre say? And then, taking the shorthand notes into his hand, he would refresh his memory; he would say, "Looking at my notes, he said so and so." Telling it in that way, and doing it in that way, reading the story from his notes, you, at the end of it, would be just as bewildered as you were at the beginning. It is impossible for you, or for anybody, to follow it in that way at all. What was done before the magistrate, and what would no doubt be the proper course before you, would be, the shorthand writer comes and says, "I was present, and took notes. I know the effect of what I did in the transcript was printed in the great blue book before me; that blue book contains a true account of it," and then that becomes evidence. You will look at that blue book and see the evidence of Mr. Eyre upon these matters. There are two different places where he gave his evidence; you shall have the pages presently. I do not know whether it is material at the present moment to point out the precise passages, but there are two places in the book where Mr. Eyre gives his evidence, and the convenient way of taking it will be, after you have heard the shorthand writers say that the transcript is correct of what Mr. Eyre did say, that you should then consider it as evidence. One word more as to the effect of the evidence. When a man makes a statement it is always, of course, evidence as against himself. You may always take a man's word in everything that makes against himself; but he is entitled, if you have any statement in evidence against him, to have the whole of what he states. If he says, I did so and so, but I did so because so and so, you cannot take a part against him without taking the part that makes for him. You are not of course bound to believe that though a man may state perfectly truly every part against him—you need not always believe that all that he said in his own favour is true; that will be a matter for you to consider. But I think probably you will come to the conclusion, from the frankness with which Mr. Eyre was speaking, that he believed he was speaking truly at the time. Further than that, when a man says, I did do this or that, it is evidence against him. When he proceeds, 'such a man told me somebody else had done something,' that would be no evidence of that something else being done, because it would be merely repeating hearsay; but it becomes very important and material evidence (if you believe him to be stating truly) as to what was told him, and what was present in his mind at the time. I wish to draw your attention to that distinction, because it is very important. The whole question really comes to be, putting yourselves in the position of Mr. Eyre, knowing all that he was told, having all the information that was brought to him; as he would not, I dare say, believe everything that was brought to him, what did he really believe and think at the time, and would that justify the acts that he did? Therefore it becomes of the greatest importance to see what Mr. Eyre was told, what he heard, and what he thought, all that was done at the time, as bringing you to the question whether or no he was guilty of that want of calmness, prudence, and self-control, which as I have said, he was bound to exercise, leading him to do those things which he might in a proper state of things have done, to such an excess, beyond what was right and proper, as to make it criminal. You will have to consider the whole that Mr. Eyre said throughout that blue book containing Mr. Eyre's evidence. The rest, of course, is not evidence. Under ordinary circumstances, I should probably give you a caution not to read further than this, but I believe that is perfectly unnecessary. I believe that in the extent of the evidence the probability is the other way. And I must give you a caution, you must read all Mr. Eyre's statement and pay attention to it all. I think when you have done that you will not have the slightest wish to read the rest. It is very long and voluminous, and very troublesome to make out. You will be rather glad when I tell you it is not your duty to do more, you are not bound to do it. You must read all that Mr. Eyre said, and consider that very carefully, but that is all.

I have just been furnished, gentlemen, with a reference to the pages in the blue book. They are no doubt accurate. They are pages 82, 981, and 1010. You will probably be furnished with copies of the blue book, but for the purpose, it is just as well to remember, that taken in addition to that, they have further produced, and will no doubt produce before you, several letters which were sent both by Mr. Eyre to the Colonial Office, and those letters are evidence for and against Mr. Eyre exactly upon the same principle and to the same extent as his verbal statements; and Mr. Eyre has in his evidence, in the frankest and openest manner, avowed what nobody can doubt, that he did proclaim martial law, and caused Mr. Gordon to be taken to Morant Bay, and there to be tried and executed, and that he did cause this martial law to continue in operation for the full period of thirty days. All that is fully avowed on his part, and I think the principal reason why your attention is wanted to these letters is, that in express terms they say, I think, that the four gentlemen whose names were mentioned, were taken in different parts of the island where martial law was not proclaimed, and sent by him to Morant Bay to be tried. That is distinctly stated in one of the letters, and I suppose it was with the object of showing that Mr. Eyre was personally concerned in that act that the letters were put in.

Further, there is parol evidence, and I must call your attention to what that is, for the purpose of making you understand the value of that evidence. The first evidence is that of Mr. Lake, who was one of the principal witnesses. He went down to Morant Bay; he was present during the earlier part, when martial law was in force, and he states what is not in the slightest degree in controversy, that martial law was then in force to a great extent, and that many persons were flogged and hanged. He further mentions a most frightful story of a Mr. Ramsay, when causing a negro to be flogged under martial law, and seeing this man under a severe flogging, gnashing his teeth, and looking either in pain or anger at the Provost-marshal who was conducting his punishment, and that Ramsay immediately ordered him to be taken on that ground, and no other, and at once hanged, and he was hanged. I need hardly tell you that if that was so a more atrocious act could not be, but I must tell you also that I have looked carefully for the purpose of seeing, and there is not, throughout the whole of the evidence, the slightest evidence that Mr. Eyre ever heard of this, not only that he did not direct it to be done, but that he never heard of it. There is always a great risk when martial law is proclaimed that there will be acts of oppression and tyranny unless it be very carefully looked at. Mr. Eyre put martial law in operation, and if this act were done it is an instance of the way in which a good many others were done; in consequence of martial law being in force, terrible things were done, but I do not think you will charge Mr. Eyre with that. There is one thing I have considered a good deal in relation to some acts. When martial law is put in force, in the sense of superseding the common law, and putting these summary powers in the hands of officers; common sense would tell a man at once that it should be very carefully looked at. The Duke of

Wellington, when he was examined before a committee, with the strong, shrewd common sense which he always possessed laid that down very strongly. He said when martial law is proclaimed, and when you have superseded common law, martial law is really the will of the commander. That was the phrase; it has been very much criticised, and it does not become that quite, but it becomes the discretion of the person exercising it; and therefore, says the Duke of Wellington (I am quoting from memory), the person in command ought to take very great care to see that it is properly regulated and controlled, and give proper directions for it. I do not think that any one can doubt that is very desirable, and I do not think in this you will have the slightest doubt, that owing to neglecting that, and letting persons run riot in the exercise of martial law, without having taken the proper care to see it rightly regulated, a vast number of things were done that ought not to have been done; and I thought then, before I knew what the charges brought were, can this be brought against Mr. Eyre as one of the charges against him? The Commissioners asked him the question, how came you not to do it? and he said, " I always considered when martial law was proclaimed I had to leave it to the military officers;" and certainly there is difficulty in saying who was responsible for this. The difficulty of the thing is this, that the duty is divided among so many; that although somebody ought to look after it there is a great difficulty in saying whose legal duty it was. Consequently, upon that view of it, I think you could not say that the failure or neglect to take proper precaution to see that martial law was fairly exercised could be charged upon Mr. Eyre, and apparently that those who conduct the prosecution have taken the same view, for they have not put any charge of that sort in the bill. They have put one charge under which it will be somewhat material for you to consider this, but this particular charge is not brought forward, and I think myself when

you see that the fault there—the fault was really great—
was in the Legislature, in not, when it originally passed
the Act, directing, that when the Governor in council did
enforce martial law throughout the country, some one,
the Governor probably, or the Commander-in-chief, should
be responsible for seeing that the martial law was fairly
and temperately exercised. It is a sort of rhetorical phrase,
but if you ' let loose the dogs of war,' you should at least
see that there is a huntsman to look after them. I think
the fault was in the Legislature; I do not think it is a
criminal offence in Mr. Eyre, although it is very much to
be lamented. Those who prepared the bill have apparently
agreed ; and have not inserted any charge of that sort.

Well, gentlemen, then you have before you one of the
persons who was imprisoned by Mr. Eyre, and taken to
Morant Bay for the purpose of being tried. He also tells
you a frightful story of what was done to him—I allude
to Phillips—about being in prison for some time, and that
he never knew what he was accused of, and was never
told. All at once he was brought out before a Mr. Adcock,
an officer there, and told he was to be flogged and dismissed. He was not told why, and he did not know why.
He was never tried, and no investigation was made. He
was very severely flogged, so as to injure his health, and
then he was dismissed. Now, if that is so, that is a case
of the most atrocious tyranny, and then, again, I say exactly as in the previous case of the man who was hanged—
I cannot find throughout the whole evidence that Mr.
Eyre in any way whatever was made aware of this, or
sanctioned it, or approved of it in any way. There is
this, that he entrusted the execution of this martial law
to those who did the act in this most atrocious manner, if
that be so, but I do not know that Mr. Eyre is brought in
connection with this matter at all.

Again, you have a witness who tells you the military
were put in operation, and marched round to cut off the
connection between the insurgents, when there was really

an insurrection in action. You have a sailor called who attended the military in their proceedings, and according to his account there was a most lamentable and terrible want of discipline, as he described it, in the way the troops marched, and shot down whom they met, for no reason except that they saw them. That shows a most lamentable want of discipline, certainly; but as to that, I think the defence of Mr. Eyre is complete, that these things were to be regulated by the military. He sent to the Commander-in-chief, "the troops must march to cut off the insurgents from getting into the other part of the island," but I do not think you will say the civil officer, the Governor, is responsible for the faults of the military. He would be if he had sent them when there was no need, or if he had sent them to do these very acts, but he is not responsible for their want of discipline. I think that parol evidence will be for you to consider, and you will see the effect of it, and I need not say anything further to guide you as to that.

I will tell you now what the charges that they are going to bring before you are. The first three counts are for proclaiming martial law; it is said that the Governor had no power to proclaim it to the extent he did; that, in fact, he would be punishable in the same way as the Mayor of London would be, or the Mayor of Bristol, at the time of the riots there. I think he would be punishable if he proclaimed martial law under circumstances where a man of firmness and moderation would not have done so, but I think, when you look at the nature of the story, as it occurred at the time martial law was proclaimed, finding that insurrection had actually arisen, that they had actually stormed the Court-house, that the Volunteers had been killed, and that they had killed the Custos, who was in the same situation as the Lord Lieutenant in England, and that they were trying to raise the country for the purpose of insurrection, I think probably you will not have the slightest hesitation in saying that you could not say that there was a want of firmness and moderation in doing it, but probably you would say if he had not done it, and he was being tried for having failed in his duty, as in the case of King and Pinney, that the circumstances were such as would have made him punishable for not doing it. It is not necessary that you should go so far as that, but I think you will not have the least hesitation in saying that he was not blameable so far as to be criminally responsible for doing it.

The next charge is more serious, that he kept this up for thirty days, when, in fact, the actual armed insurrection had been stopped after the first day or two, and that he kept it up to a very great extent, and in a manner in which he was not authorized to do, whether there was criminal excess in doing it so long and so much. Now, upon that, the nature of the want of control of this exercise of martial law does come into consideration here. If those who had been exercising martial law had been well held in hand, as they would have been by the Duke of Wellington, had he been in command, if they had been moderate, calm, and temperate, very much slighter things would have justified the keeping it up for the full period of thirty days. He might then have said, We will keep up the power, and keep it well in control and well in hand, so as to have the power, though we will not exercise it, except in case of need; then, I think, comparatively little would have justified a man of calmness and moderation in still keeping it up for the purpose of having control in case of need; but when you find martial law is exercised, as it undoubtedly was, in a very wild and reckless manner, and to a degree which you must form your own opinion of, because I am not giving you directions in point of law here, but assisting you as to the facts,—when you find it was exercised to a degree which was more than was necessary for the purpose of stopping the insurrection,—then comes the question whether the circumstances which came

H

then to Mr. Eyre's knowledge were such as to make him
criminally responsible for that excess. It is first for you
to say if it was an excess, in fact; I am inclined to say so
myself. Then you are to say whether it was such an excess, putting yourselves in Mr. Eyre's position, as to make
him criminally responsible. Upon that, I only say this, that
there is evidence upon which you would be fully justified
in saying that it was, and there is evidence upon which
you would be fully justified in saying that the circumstances were such as to make it not so. It is rather a
question of the inference you draw. You may consider
on the one hand that martial law had been properly proclaimed by the advice of the full council, consisting of all
those persons that I have named, and you will consider,
again, whether Mr. Eyre was justified or not in what he
did; taking into consideration that he had before him
evidence and statements from all parts of the country that
they apprehended insurrection, and dreaded that it would
spread through the country, and I think you will see
that he had come to the conclusion that there was an
organised conspiracy. I do not think the evidence leads
me to the conclusion that that really was so, but I am far
from saying that Mr. Eyre might not have honestly
thought so. Then martial law had been already proclaimed, and the question comes to him, Shall I stop it,
or not? If I stop it, and the country is exposed to the
dreadful effects of the insurrection, I shall have done very
great mischief. He would be then responsible for that
mischief, and might, perhaps, be accused, and made criminally responsible for it. I pass by what might be said of
Mr. Eyre, how he might be accused and punished for it.
I think the question, whether he was to keep it up or not
depends very much, indeed, upon the extent to which you
think a man of firmness, and calmness, and moderation
would really believe that unless the summary process of
martial law was kept up there would be great danger in
other places. I have already told you that he would be

justified in it if it was absolutely necessary for the purpose of stopping and suppressing the insurrection, but I do not think it would be if it was not. Then you are to put yourselves in his position, and make all due allowance for his position, not making too much, but all due allowance, and say whether, under those circumstances, he did bring that amount of ordinary firmness, calmness, and moderation to the consideration of the question which he ought to have done; and, if he did act honestly in that way, whether his failure to act with the necessary degree of firmness and moderation was to such an extent as to make it a criminal failure, which, as I have already said, is an indefinite phrase, but one that you must bring common sense to bear upon.

Then come further charges, that he took Mr. Gordon in Kingston, where he might have been safely kept, that he imprisoned him there and then took him and imprisoned him on board the Wolverine, and carried him to Morant Bay, to be tried by martial law there, which they say was tyrannical and oppressive. I have already told you, and I need not repeat it, my view—If the motive, the object, was the indirect and improper one, it would be an act of very great tyranny and oppression; but if you come to the conclusion, that it really was done honestly under the belief that Mr. Gordon was really guilty, and not only really guilty, but that the conspiracy was an organised and extended one, and that at the time he did it there was very great danger and risk of the conspiracy breaking out throughout the country, and that causing him to be tried and executed was an essential measure for stopping that insurrection, if you think—taking a proper degree of calmness and fairness to bear upon that question—he thought so; he would not be guilty upon this charge. I merely say to you that there is evidence proper to be considered and weighed by you. I think upon that evidence, according to the inference you draw from it, you may fairly find the charge, or you may fairly not find that charge. Then the same may be said with respect to each of the other cases of those who were taken out of the proclaimed district. There is a charge that Mr. Eyre caused two of them to be flogged. I do not see the evidence of one of them being flogged in a summary way. The other, Mr. Phillips, tells us the frightful story of what would be most improper, and tyrannical, and oppressive; but I have looked through the evidence in vain to see that Mr. Eyre sanctioned or authorised, or even knew of it. He sent him to Morant Bay to be tried, and to be kept in custody, but I cannot find that he directed these very wrongful proceedings to be done, and I cannot find, therefore, anything to make him responsible for that. If you find that there is any evidence that he did sanction it—it may have escaped my notice in the blue-book—it would be an act that could not be at all justified or excused; and so as to the act of Ramsay's (if you believe it) in taking the man to be hanged. These things may have a bearing upon the question whether Mr. Eyre, in keeping up martial law so long, was acting properly, because if you find martial law was exercised in such a way as to make such things possible, that would bear upon the question you have to consider.

Now, gentlemen, I have done, I think, everything I can to help you in this case. You have to consider the matter carefully, because it only requires that you should tell me whether you find a bill in part or in whole, or whether you do not find a bill. You will tell me, some time during term. You will have to get all the evidence before you, and you will find, I think, when you come to look at the case, that the great question, and the important question for you, will be carefully to draw your own inference as to what really were the circumstances and position of Jamaica—how things came to Mr. Eyre's mind in Jamaica in the very difficult position in which he was,. and whether or no there was criminal excess in the sense I have pointed out. The greater part of what I have said latterly is to help and assist you, not to direct

you. You will have to determine the question of fact for
yourselves upon your own responsibility, I am glad to say
it is not mine. I think I have had responsibility enough
in the case, and I have no wish to take any part of it from
you. You will decide these matters for yourselves. There
is only one other matter that I should mention, merely
that it should not be supposed I have omitted it. Subsequent to these proceedings the Jamaica Legislature passed
an Act, which has been allowed by the Government as an
indemnity, and no doubt a contention will be made hereafter, in case you find the bill, that the existence of that
indemnity would be a bar to proceedings in this Court:
and, if that were clear, it would be a reason for throwing
out the bill: for you are not to harass a man when there
is a clear defence. I do not wish to express any opinion
now as to whether or not that Act would apply. There
is a doubt in my mind, which is a very grave and
serious one, whether, when an act has been done which,
according to the Imperial Legislature, would be triable as
a crime in England, and when you have, as it were, a
vested interest in trying that crime, whether the colonial
Legislature, although supreme in the colony, could undo
that crime which had become punishable by law here.
In one view, I take it, the law is pretty clear, that
after a bill had been found here, it would not have
been competent to the Jamaica Legislature to pass any
Act of Indemnity, equivalent to a pardon. I do not
wish to express an opinion whether the colonial legislature are competent or not to set aside the right to
find a bill which existed in England. Supposing you
think the facts bear it out, I only say that is a point that
will be argued hereafter in case you find the bill, and it is
one upon which a good deal may be said on both sides. I
do not wish in the slightest degree to prejudge it. I only
mention that in order that you may disregard it altogether.
Taking the guide I have given you, and applying your
own sense to the evidence, if you think there is ground for

putting Mr. Eyre on his trial by finding a bill for excess of duty in the way I have explained to you, then find a bill, leaving him to the Act of Indemnity afterwards. But if you come to the conclusion that it is not so, and, looking at the evidence, and, taking the law from me, you do not think there is ground for charging him, you will be justified in acting on that view, as I have stated. If you come to the conclusion that there is not a case of criminal excess of duty for which he ought to be punished, you may throw out the bill, or you may find the bill upon part of the charge and reject it as to part, if you think the facts of the case require you to do it.

Now I have done; I have nothing further to say to you, except that you will retire to your room, and make your own arrangements for the purpose of taking the evidence, and considering it, and when you have considered it calmly and clearly, you will tell me, or rather the Court of Queen's Bench, what is the result, whether you find the bill or not, or whether you throw it out altogether. I have no doubt you will bring your own minds carefully to consider the question, and whatever result you arrive at I am sure will be perfectly honest, and quite satisfactory.

The grand jury ignored the bill.

APPENDIX.

IN THE QUEEN'S BENCH, JUNE 8TH, 1868.

Before the Lord Chief Justice and Justice Lush.

A WEEK after the foregoing charge had been delivered and published to the world, the following observations were made by the Lord Chief Justice, which will be found to have arisen entirely from his not observing the distinction so carefully drawn by the learned Judge between *matter of law*, and its practical application to a particular case, the former involving general propositions for the Judge; the latter, mixed propositions of law and fact, applicable to a particular case, which are for the jury. The learned Judge had strictly confined himself to the former. The Lord Chief Justice, not observing this, had supposed that as he himself, in his charge in Nelson's case, had assumed that his province included the latter, the learned Judge had done so. But the learned Judge had laid down only *matters of law;* and it will be found that in what follows there is no dissent from any proposition of law laid down, and that there is a distinct assent to propositions of law which legally and logically involve *every* matter of law he laid down. The utmost that the Lord Chief Justice does is to express a doubt as to one or two matters, and to express dissent from a mixed proposition of law and fact which the learned Judge never laid down at all, and which would not be within the province of a judge. It need hardly be added that, as the case was at an end, the whol of the observations were entirely extra-judicial, and of no judicial authority whatever, beyond the mere correction of a mistake as to the extent which the Court had *concurred.* The expression of *dissent*, or the exposition of grounds of dissent, would be entirely extra-judicial. But, as already observed, there is no decided dissent *from any proposition of law.* And there is a decided *assent* to propositions of law which legally and logically involve everything the learned Judge laid down. So that the effect is, though indirectly, to enhance the authority of the charge, by confirming the statement of the learned Judge, that it had, as to the matters of law laid down, the *assent of the whole Court.*

THE LORD CHIEF JUSTICE.—Before we proceed with the regular business of the Court, I feel it necessary to say a few words upon a subject which appears to me too important to be passed over in silence, though it does not arise on any matter which is now before us. It has gone forth to the world, that, in the charge recently delivered by my brother Blackburn to the Grand Jury of the County of Middlesex, in the case of Regina v. Eyre, the law laid down by the learned Judge, in his direction to the jury, had received the assent and approbation of the other members of this Court. I regret to say that there has been a very serious misapprehension on this point, and I think it due, not only to the Court and myself, but also to the profession and the public, that this misapprehension should be cleared up at the earliest moment, and that it should be understood how far the legal doctrines enunciated on the occasion in question have the sanction and authority of the Court.

There was undoubtedly a proposition of law which seemed to us sufficient for the guidance of the jury, and which we understood was to form (if I may so express myself) the basis of the charge, on which proposition we were all agreed, namely, that assuming the Governor of a colony had, by virtue of authority delegated to him by the Crown, or conferred upon him by local legislation, the power to put martial law in force, all that could be required of him, so far as affects his responsibility in a Court of Criminal Law, was that, in judging of the necessity which it is admitted on all hands affords the sole justification for resorting to martial law, either for putting this exceptional law in force or prolonging its duration, he should not only act with an honest intention to discharge a public duty, but should bring to the consideration of the course to be pursued the careful, conscientious and considerate judgment which may reasonably be expected from one invested with authority, and which, in our opinion, a Governor so circumstanced is bound to exercise before he places the Queen's subjects committed to his government beyond the pale of protection of the law.

Having done this, he would not be liable for error of judgment, and still less for excesses or irregularities committed by subordinates whom he is under the necessity of employing, if committed without his sanction or knowledge.

Furthermore, we consider that a Governor sworn to execute the laws of a colony, if advised by those competent to advise him that those laws justify him in proclaiming martial law in the manner in which Governor Eyre understood it, cannot be held criminally responsible if the circumstances call for its exercise, and though it should afterwards turn out that the received opinion as to the law was erroneous. On the other hand, in the absence of such careful and conscientious exercise and judgment, mere honesty of intention would be no excuse for a reckless, precipitate, and inconsiderate exercise of so formidable a power, still less for any abuse of it in regard to the lives and persons of Her Majesty's subjects, or in the application of immoderate severity in excess of what the exigencies of the occasion imperatively called for. Neither could the continuance of martial law be exercised, even as regards criminal responsibility, when the necessity which can alone justify it had ceased by the entire suppression of all insurrection, either for the purpose of punishing those who were suspected of having been concerned in it, or of striking terror into the minds of men for the time to come.

This was the substance of what we all concurred in thinking was the proper direction to be given to the jury, as to the responsibility of the Governor in applying or continuing martial law. This was all which appeared to us necessary to lay down in point of law ; all that remained was to apply the law thus laid down to the facts and circumstances of the case : on the one hand, to the formidable character of the insurrection, and the terrible consequences that might have ensued to the white population in the event of a rising of the negroes becoming general ; on the other hand, to the fact of the immediate suppression of the insurrection, and to the prolongation of martial law for several weeks after order and tranquillity had been perfectly restored, to the fearful number of executions that took place, and the terrible punishments which had been inflicted during this period ; leaving it to the jury to consider whether what had been done was what reason and humanity could justify. And not only was the legal doctrine to which I have referred all that the rest of the Court in fact assented to ; but I feel justified in saying that it was all that they expected would be embraced in the charge, as necessary for the guidance of the jury. Therefore, as either through misconception on the part of the learned judge, or from the language of the charge not being sufficiently precise, an erroneous impression has been created that the Court has sanctioned all the legal positions asserted in the charge ; and as it is in the last degree important that in a matter where great constitutional principles are involved doctrines should not go forth as stamped with the sanction of this high court of criminal judicature when no such sanction has in fact been given, I thought it my duty to point out the error which has arisen, and to declare the extent to which alone the assent of the Court must be considered as having gone, but so far as I am individually concerned I must go further, and declare that there are in the charge of the learned Judge, as it has appeared in print (and I have no other means of information) propositions of law in which I not only am not prepared to concur, but from which I altogether dissent. I differ, in the first place, from the learned judge in the conclusion at which he seems to have arrived, that martial law, in the modern acceptation of the term, was ever exercised in this country, at all events with any pretence of legality, against civilians not taken in arms. The instance referred to is of a most doubtful character.

In the second place, while I have never doubted that it was competent to the Legislature of Jamaica to confer upon the Governor the power to put martial law in force, I entertain, for reasons I have stated elsewhere, very great doubts whether the Jamaica statutes have any reference to martial law, except for the purpose of compelling the inhabitants of the island to military service, and subjecting them while engaged in it to military law. I abstain from expressing any positive opinion on so débateable a question, but I must at the same time say, that, in my judgment there is too much doubt upon the subject to warrant a judge, in the absence of argument at the bar, and judicial decision, to direct a grand jury authoritatively that these statutes warrant the application of martial law. Nor does such a direction appear to me to be at all necessary, seeing that we are agreed that a governor giving effect to these statutes in the sense in which they have been understood in the colony would not be criminally responsible.

But above all, I dissent from the direction of my brother Blackburn as reported, in telling the Grand Jury that the removal of Mr. Gordon from Kingston into the proclaimed district for the purpose of subjecting him to martial law was legally justifiable. I emphatically repudiate the notion of sharing that opinion.

I have felt it to be my duty to advert to these things, not only for the purpose of clearing up the impression as to the extent to which the other members are pledged to the doctrines contained in the charge, but also because clearly of the opinion that the collective authority of the Court is pledged in every charge delivered to the Grand Jury of Middlesex in the Court of Queen's Bench. When the senior Puisne Judge of this Court delivers, in pursuance of long-established custom, a charge to the Grand Jury of Middlesex, the charge he so delivers is that of the Court, and not that of the single judge who pronounces it. He speaks not of his own authority, or on his sole responsibility alone, he is the organ and mouthpiece of the Court, and I am therefore clearly of opinion that in the event of any difference of opinion as to the direction to be given to a grand jury, it will be the right, as well as the duty, of each judge to be present and to deliver his own charge as in the case of a trial at bar.

Assuredly had I known that the law would have been laid down as it is understood to have been stated, I should have felt it to be my duty to attend in my place in Court on the occasion of the charge being delivered, and to declare my view of the law to the jury. I must add, as my justification for not having done so, that I certainly understood from the learned Judge, though I must now suppose that I must have misunderstood him, that he deemed it unnecessary to raise the question of the legality of the martial law or the effect of the Jamaica statutes; and as regards the very serious case of Mr. Gordon, I believe I am right in saying that almost to the eve of the delivery of the charge, the opinion of my brother Blackburn himself was that the apprehension and removal of Mr. Gordon were in point of law unjustifiable, and certainly was so understood by other members of the Court, and I believe I am warranted in saying that the statement of the learned Judge to the Grand Jury on this head took the other members of the Court as much by surprise as it certainly took me. Had I been led to expect that in a charge delivered in my own Court my opinion declared to the Grand Jury in the case of the Queen *v.* Nelson and

Brand would have been thus authoritatively overruled, I should certainly have deemed it my duty to declare my own opinion to the Grand Jury, and to apprise them that the statement of the law thus made to them had not the sanction of any other member of the Court besides that of the learned judge who made it.

It is not without much pain, and only under an imperious sense of public duty, that I make these observations. The Bar have now known me too long, I hope, to misconstrue my motives, or to believe that in doing so I am actuated by any vain desire to uphold my own opinions against those of any other judge, or from any sensitiveness at having opinions or my doubts which I have judicially expressed, ignored, or overruled. I am influenced only by the desire of protecting myself against being held responsible for opinions from which I dissent, and of preventing doctrines going forth stamped with the authority of this the highest Court of criminal jurisdiction in the realm, the House of Lords alone excepted, to which that assent has not been given. It may be that at some future time, I trust it may be far distant, the question as to the exercise of martial law may again present itself when we who are now the members of the Court shall be no longer here to assert and vindicate our opinions. In that event the charge of so disinterested a Judge as my brother Blackburn would, from his judicial position and known attainments no doubt be referred to; and, but for the course I have now felt it necessary to take, the whole of the law thus laid down might be taken to have been declared with the sanction of this Court. In such a case I hope that what I have now said may be remembered, and will prevent any misconception on the subject. It may be, too, that it may operate as a salutary warning to those who, being placed in authority, may proceed to exercise martial law, to know that an act such as the seizure of Mr. Gordon was, in the opinion of a majority of the Judges of this Court, altogether unjustifiable and illegal: and that there are those who consider that a Governor or other authority, in putting martial law in force, or continuing it, or in the degree of severity exercised under it, is responsible to the law if he acts otherwise than under a sense of imperious and impending necessity, or without a due regard to what reason and humanity alike require.

Mr. JUSTICE BLACKBURN :—I do not intend to make any observations whatever either as to what was the direction I gave to the Grand Jury in this case, or as to the accuracy of that direction in point of law, but to take this opportunity of correcting any misapprehension which exists as to the extent to which the charge represents the opinions of more Judges than one. I never intended to say that any one else was responsible in the least for the observations which, by way of affording assistance to the Grand Jury, I made on the evidence, to enable them to apply the law laid down to what they might find to be the facts. No one can form any opinion on such matters without having studied the whole evidence, and the bearing of each part on the rest, and I could not, and did not, ask any one to undertake that very laborious task in the present case. I thought I had so expressed myself as to show that I alone was responsible for what was said as to the application of the law to the particular parts of the case. But if any one has fallen into any misapprehension as to this, I am happy to take this opportunity of correcting it. With regard to the points of law the case is different; I consider myself bound to direct the jury according to my own view of the law, but also bound to take every means in my power to secure my view of the law should be a correct one. I need only say that with that object I read carefully the Lord Chief Justice's charge in the case of the Queen against Nelson and Brand. I came to the conclusion, it may be an erroneous one, but one which I still entertain, that there was no part on which it was necessary to give the Grand Jury a direction on which my opinion as to the law was in conflict with any direction contained in that charge. On the Monday when I had finally arranged my ideas, I stated to the Lord Chief Justice and to my brother Judges of the Court of Queen's Bench, the heads of what I proposed to lay before the Grand Jury as the law to guide them. The propositions which I considered the most important, namely, as to the principle on which the criminal responsibility in a governor or other officer charged with the duty of putting down an insurrection depended, I had reduced to writing. The others, applicable to the particular points in the case, I stated briefly, but, as I thought, sufficiently to explain them. They approved of what I stated, and the Lord Chief Justice said if I thought it would give more weight to what I was about to say, I might tell the Grand Jury that they did approve of them; I was highly pleased, and not doubting that it would add very greatly to the weight of my direction as to what the law was, I did tell the Grand Jury. I now perceive that I ought to have remembered that my mind was full of what I had been deliberating upon, and that though what I said seemed to me to be a full statement of what I was about to tell the jury, it by no means followed that it was understood as fully as I supposed and intended. I ought to have taken more care to ascertain that there was no misunderstanding as to this. Had this occurred to me in time I should still have felt bound to deliver the same direction to the jury, telling them that it was what I considered the law and therefore was to guide them, I alone being responsible for it, but that direction would have gone forth to the profession and the country as having no more weight than was to be attached to my own individual opinion, conscientiously, deliberately, and laboriously formed, but still mine only. Under a misapprehension it went forth as entitled to much greater weight. As soon as I learnt there was a misapprehension I was anxious to correct it, and I now take this opportunity of doing so.

THE LORD CHIEF JUSTICE.—I thought all that I heard, or was asked about, was the proposition with regard to the responsibility of Governor Eyre in substance, I will not say in terms, but in substance as I have stated them.

EXTRACTS FROM THE CHARGE OF THE LORD CHIEF JUSTICE IN NELSON'S CASE.

As in the foregoing observations of the Lord Chief Justice it should seem that he was under the impression that he had laid down some matters of law in Nelson's case, and especially as that his expression of opinion in that charge as to Gordon's removal, that it was unlawful and unjustifiable, was a legal proposition, instead of being, as it is conceived, an extra-judicial expression of opinion upon a matter of fact, or mixed law and fact, properly for the jury, entirely irrelevant to the question before him ; utterly unwarranted by the evidence, and indeed, contrary to it ; and, as extremely prejudicial to a party, Mr. Eyre not being before him any way, altogether "unlawful and unjustifiable," it may be proper here to give extracts from his charge, showing that neither as to that matter, nor any other, was there any proposition of law in the charge at all. The indictment, in that case, was against Colonel Nelson for the trial and execution, he having nothing to do with the *removal*. So that, to begin with, the matter was irrelevant. In the next place, the only *evidence* before him was that of Colonel Nelson, whose statements were put in, and who stated that Mr. Eyre desired *him* to "examine the evidence, to see if it was sufficient, and to have Gordon tried if it *was* sufficient, and if it was proper, in his view, to have him tried." (Minutes of Evid., pp. 622—625.) That was the *evidence before the Lord Chief Justice*, upon which he said to the Grand Jury that those gentlemen, the Governor and Custos, had no power derived from the military authorities to take up this man for the purpose of handing him over to the martial law. That was, it will be observed, no proposition of law, though it probably appeared to the Grand Jury to be one. And the Lord Chief Justice never laid it down as a proposition of law that removal into a district under martial law is necessarily illegal. That would have been a legal proposition ; but he has nowhere laid it down, and it would be clearly contrary to the opinion of the twelve Judges in Lundy's case. (See Review of the Authorities.) But he merely said that the Governor had no power "*derived from the military authorities*" to remove the man. And then he went on to say to the Grand Jury—the evidence before him being that Mr. Eyre had submitted to the military commander whether the evidence was sufficient, and had desired that the man should not be tried unless it was so :—

"They did it by the strong hand of power. Indeed it has been avowed, and the motive of it has been avowed, viz., that it was *thought that a conviction could not be got at Kingston, therefore* they took him from Kingston, where there was no martial law, and where he was safe, to Morant Bay, where there was martial law, and where *a military tribunal could be found to try, and condemn him.*" (Charge, p. 114.)

Now, then, upon that, the Lord Chief Justice immediately added :—

"I entertain the very strong opinion that the whole proceeding—the seizing him, and handing him over to the martial tribunal—was altogether unlawful and unjustifiable." (Ibid.)

This is what the Lord Chief Justice appears to have been anxious to repeat, as if it were a proposition of law. It is for the reader to judge whether it was not wholly extra-judicial, and, being extremely prejudicial to an absent man, "altogether unlawful and unjustifiable." But at all events, it was not a proposition of law. It was a mere expression of opinion on a mixed proposition of law and fact, which was for the jury, if it had been relevant. But it was, as the Lord Chief Justice went on to show, quite irrelevant, For, he said—

"It does *not affect the question we are now considering*, viz., whether, having been brought within the ambit of the martial law, he *was liable to be tried under it. I cannot but think he was.*" (Ibid., p. 119.)

So that, if the strong expression of opinion had been on matter of law, it was entirely irrelevant, and so quite extra-judicial. But it will be manifest it was entirely a matter of fact, for it went upon the *suggested conspiracy to condemn the man without evidence*, which was assuredly a question of fact, had it been relevant, and had there been the least foundation for it. But the Lord Chief Justice himself said it was irrelevant, and showed it was unfounded. For he had said :—

"It was *believed by the authorities* that Mr. Gordon had been the instigator of the rebellion, and an accomplice with those who were actually engaged in it. It was therefore *thought right and necessary* to make him answerable *for the offences of which it was believed he had been guilty.*" (Ibid., p. 7.)

No lawyer can entertain a doubt that a strong expression of opinion, resting on a matter of fact, as to the conduct of *an absent individual*, not only *without*, but *contrary* to, the evidence, entirely irrelevant, and extremely prejudicial—so far from having any judicial authority, was, on the contrary, utterly extra-judicial, and "altogether unlawful and unjustifiable." Yet, it will have been observed, that this *was the only point upon which, in the foregoing observations, the Lord Chief Justice expressed any decided view*, except in *accordance* with the law laid down by Mr. Justice Blackburn. And that, in his charge, the Lord Chief Justice *laid down no legal proposition*, will be manifest from the terms in which he left the case, in conclusion, to the Grand Jury :—

"It may be, that all I have said upon the subject of the law, will have left you, as I own candidly it still leaves me, in some degree of doubt. Let me, therefore, add, that *if you are of opinion that the jurisdiction to exercise martial law is not made out*, I think the safer course will be to let the matter go forward. If, however, upon *the review of the authorities* to which I have called your attention, and of the enactment in the Jamaica statutes, you think the accused ought not further to be harassed by criminal proceedings, you will say so by ignoring this indictment. Upon that *you must exercise your own judgment.*" (Charge, p. 10.)

Thus, therefore, the matter of law was left to the jury, and there was no judicial direction to them upon it, and *no legal propositions were laid down at all.* So that Mr. Justice Blackburn was quite right in saying that there was no difference in the *law* as laid down by the Lord Chief Justice and himself.

www.ingramcontent.com/pod-product-compliance
Lightning Source LLC
Chambersburg PA
CBHW030333170426
43202CB00010B/1112